TWO
FRIENDS
IN
LOVE

ED & CAROL NEUENSCHWANDER

MULTNOMAH • PRESS

Portland, Oregon 97266

Unless otherwise indicated, all Scripture references are from the New American Standard Bible, © The Lockman Foundation 1960, 1962, 1963, 1968, 1971, 1972, 1973, 1975, 1977. Used by permission.

Scripture references marked TLB are taken from The Living Bible, copyright 1971 by Tyndale House Publishers, Wheaton, Ill.

Cover design: Michael Standlee
Photograph: Robert Nease

Edited by Jane E. Aldrich

TWO FRIENDS IN LOVE

Portland, Oregon 97266
Printed in the United States of America

Library of Congress Cataloging-in-Publication Data
Neuenschwander, Ed.
Two friends in love.

Includes bibliographical references.
1. Marriage—Religious aspects—Christianity.
I. Neuenschwander, Carol. II. Title. III. Title:
2 friends in love.
BV835.N48 1986 248.8'4 85-28402
ISBN 0-88070-121-8 (pbk.)

85 86 87 88 89 90 – 10 9 8 7 6 5 4 3 2 1

To our parents

Ed and Juanita Neuenschwander
and
Ken and Ann Siemen

who have stood faithfully with us
these past nineteen years of our lives
and have shown us what it is
to never stop growing together.

Contents

Foreword

The words of Sir Francis Bacon often come to my mind when I pick up a pen to do some writing: "Reading maketh a broad man. Speaking, a ready man. Writing, an exact man." My two friends, Ed and Candee Neuenschwander, who wrote the book you are about to read, qualify as broad, ready, exact people. Both know the value of being well-read individuals, both are engaged in publicly sharing what they have learned in their long-term marriage, and now both have put their ideas into print. I am proud of their achievement, but more than that, I am impressed with the quality of their lives.

The Neuenschwanders and the Swindolls have a friendship that stretches back to 1971. Our lives have been interwoven in ministry for more than a dozen years, both at the church I pastor and in a radio ministry I'm a part of. We have reared busy families together (both of us have four children, each with two boys and two girls), camped together, eaten together, laughed and loved together, wept and struggled together, dreamed and planned together, grown and learned together.

Not too many months ago our lives were separated from each other as Ed and his family moved many miles away when he became the senior pastor of a fine church in northern California. He and Candee were well underway with their book by then and I urged them to finish it, regardless of the interruptions that were sure to occur. I had read enough of it by then to realize its value in the lives of married couples today.

Foreword

In our day of superficiality, authenticity is rare. In our day of knowledge, wisdom is unusual. In our day of shallow relationships and throw-away marriage, long-lasting commitment is lacking. In our day of cheap talk about sex, marital romance is virtually unheard of. In our day of mutual frustrations and husband-wife competition, the cultivation of a harmonious friendship in the home seems too idealistic to mention. In our day of deceit, dishonesty, and disapproval between partners, the much-needed presence of honesty and understanding is conspicuous by its absence.

But instead of criticizing and complaining about what terrible times these are, this couple has decided to take a much more positive stance. With a great deal of scriptural support and practical insight, they have gone beneath the symptomatic surface and addressed the crucial issues that lead to weakness and disease in marriage. Then with wisdom and skill they have provided realistic prescriptions that will bring back to health and happiness a relationship that has come dangerously near death. What they suggest isn't easy and won't come naturally (it certainly isn't being followed by the majority), but it will work.

I know that for a fact. As proof, I can name at least one couple whose marriage is a model of these principles. Their work is a balanced blend of Bacon's words, and their lives are as creative and tasteful as the book you now have the privilege of reading—Ed and Candee Neuenschwander.

Charles R. Swindoll, Senior Pastor
First Evangelical Free Church of Fullerton, California
Radio Bible Teacher, Insight for Living

Preface

This book comes to you because of our commitment to the well-being of our own marriage and a concern for marriages around us which are showing signs of struggle. As we've read works available to us and others today, we've come to realize that there is much more to be said about marriage and the problems we each face than has yet been written. We know this volume is but a portion of what still needs to be said about questions confronting us as we try to keep together marriages we cherish.

To make this book more readable for you, we have chosen to put it in the first person active voice, with Ed being the speaker and Carol—Candee to family and friends—standing in the background. However, both of us have contributed equally to making the book what it is.

Thanks for taking this book in hand and perusing it with the intent of bettering your relationship with your mate. Our prayer for you is that you will think deeply about the questions we raise and the answers we offer. We want you to know the same kind of joy in your marriage that we have found within our own.

Ed and Candee Neuenschwander

We want to thank Chuck and Cynthia Swindoll
who believed in us in our formative years of family life
and who served as a continuous inspiration to this project;
to our children—Heather, Joy, Tim and Jonothan—
who showed interest in what we were doing;
and to Jane Aldrich and the staff at Multnomah who
took our work and handled it with both
excellence and heart.

1

Growing Together:

The Result of a Carefully Made Choice

The fire crackled contentedly, casting a warm glow over the room. Couples nestled on the couches, others on the floor. The atmosphere was relaxed and intimate. My wife Candee and I had been a part of this scene for the past several years, sharing our home and lives with couples who were interested in bettering their marriages. We talked about our marital friendships and why romance often dies. We discussed the ways relationships suffer while bowing to jobs and recreation, to child rearing and family responsibilities, and to a wide variety of stresses to which we were all exposed. We were there to construct solutions that would carry us from weakness to strength, that would help us win! None of us wanted to lose by default.

While considering some fresh thoughts on how to help ourselves beyond mere duty, to give our promises to each other more depth and vitality, Jack broke an uncharacteristic silence. He put it like this:

> I am beginning to see that when I married Karen I committed myself to the borders of our union. And not understanding the need to make our commitment more specific than that, we have both hung in there with the duty part of keeping our vows while the joy of our relationship has eluded us. I am now seeing that my commitment to her needs to be broader. I need to extend my pledge to keeping our friendship alive, and I must give priority to the growth of our romance.

You see, Jack had been doing what so many are doing. He was faithful to Karen, and he was being careful not to let his affections wander outside the fence of his vows. But life inside that fence had become weak. Thus, when he made a commitment to growth and a new set of choices, the tone of his marriage began to change.

If you want to make the most of your life and marriage, then you must make firm choices that will produce the enduring growth you want and need, as Jack did. I ask you, is your marriage long on duty and short on growth, friendship, and romance? Are you searching for something that will deepen your love roots into each other's lives?

Hope and Intention Are Not Enough

For the most part we marry with the hope and intention of sticking together for life. Bill and Arlene, like so many of us, however, found that wasn't enough. Their courtship was special. Both had mild, pleasant dispositions. Seemingly without effort, they displayed a sweet manner toward each other that was contagious. It affected me.

They had much in common. In fact, they believed *that* alone would put their marriage yards ahead of those of their peers. As is my custom in the premarital counseling process, I asked them, "Why do you both have confidence your marriage will survive?"

Looking at one another, smiling as they looked back at me, Bill replied on their behalf. "Because we have a strong hope it will work, and we have every intention of seeing that it survives." He glanced at her, she smiled in confirmation, and they clasped hands more tightly and inched closer together.

One afternoon four years later I was sitting quietly in my office when my secretary poked her head in the door and asked, "Take a call from Bill?" When I picked up the phone and greeted him, he began:

> Ed, I don't know if you've heard. Arlene took our little guys and left home last month. Soon after our honeymoon, conflicts arose that we thought would fade in time. We hadn't expected them, though you'd told us they would come. Before long, talking about them was difficult . . . soon impossible. I know this has shocked our friends. We now see that we need more than hope and intention to make things work, and we are faced with a decision: Are we going to make the choices that will draw us together and help us overcome our selfish patterns? Where do we go from here? We're at a serious and intense impasse.

Sad to say, only one wanted to try again. The other had given up. Growing demanded work and energy . . . even forgiveness. And one felt that was too much to ask in view of their past. The original bubbly friendship was eroded, and a fundamental reason for keeping their marriage alive had washed away. Though the marriage could have been rescued, it wasn't.

An alternative is needed for building or reestablishing a marital relationship—an alternative that preserves the integrity of both the husband and the wife and protects the friendship that first prompted the decision to get married. The purpose of this book is to offer you such an alternative.

Often when we sense failure in a marriage, it leads to disillusionment. Hope and intention can unravel. And before long, mates can become intensely preoccupied with the downside of their love affair.

We often believe in our impressionable years that good marriages are essentially problem free. The love-conquers-all theory. But veterans of marriage—good marriages included—can testify to the reality that marriage, like all other relationships, contains unavoidable snags and chuckholes, each one needing examination and repair.

Marriages are troubled because imperfect individuals come together and form imperfect unions. Yours is no exception and neither is mine. A marriage simply will not be any more trouble free than the humans who constitute it.

Hope and intention just aren't enough to keep mates together for a lifetime. Bill and Arlene stand among a choir of others singing that tune. If a marriage is going to outpace its troubles and conflicts, a carefully made choice is necessary. We must choose to do those things and develop those responses that provide it with life and security. *We must choose to grow together* our entire shared life. Then we must routinely make additional supporting choices to keep that initial choice alive and moving forward.

The Impact of Other Marriages on Your Own

Look into your own experience a moment. Do you find yourself at times peering over your shoulder, questioning your own chances for survival? Do you wonder if your ability to have a successful marriage is as strong as you'd thought it to be? Have the collapsing marriages of friends and business associates, of brothers, sisters, or perhaps parents instilled fear in you that you too might fail?

If so, you are not alone. All too frequently when a union close to us stumbles, its fall can bruise our hope; then fear begins to gnaw at our soul. It is often in this climate of uncertainty that we live our married lives. This uncertain atmosphere hangs above us like a thick, gray cloud, darkening our hope for survival.

Fear and uncertainty seem to slug hard when things *appear* to be irreconcilable. Notice, I emphasize *appear.* Fear can distort what's actually there. And during conflict it can become difficult to find even strands of confidence and intimacy to hold us together, strands that were plentiful in the early days of friendship. This happened with Bill and Arlene.

Viral Insecurity . . . It Touches Us All

Just as our bodies are upset by viral infections of a broad sort, our emotions—and thus our marriages—are periodically touched and affected by insecurity. At times it's only short-lived. Sometimes it lingers. It is no respecter of persons. A couple may live content, thoroughly happy. Then without notice the bug hits one of them. Since our environment is laden with insecurity, we can't always escape its influence on our marriage affairs.

Most of us are inclined to feel awkward in our love anyway. We don't even need to watch troubled marriages stumble beside us to have insecurity, for plenty of it lurks in the cracks of our own relationships. This nuisance can appear when we're hurriedly shoved between the passages of life, where the rude and inconsiderate effects of aging strip us of our youth—especially when one of us ages more quickly than the other, or as one person's health fades and the other person's holds its own. Retirement, premature or otherwise, often ignites it. And that which touches us personally influences the security of our love, which through the years is battered about by stresses and disappointments of all sorts.

It is in this context we must choose to grow.

Growth Demands Tough Choices

The survival or death of your marriage during all the seasons of life will be determined by the tough, sometimes feelingless choices you make. In today's world we must grow if we are going to cope.

As an individual, it is your job to see that you grow. As a couple, you must be custodians of your shared development and progress. And beyond that, you must see to it that your growth is both broad and balanced . . . that it is being achieved on all fronts.

You might inwardly resist that, saying, "Why can't we simply be left alone to live? We'll be okay if you give us enough time and space. The problems will work themselves out." But realistically, they don't! Couples who've chosen that approach over the years have lost. Growth is a stranger to passivity, and a friend only to diligence.

Growth often comes as a byproduct of pain and difficulty, but with it comes great satisfaction. Think about it this way:

The pain of discipline is greater than the pain of regret. Therefore if you want your marriage to be something special, something above average, then you must start by making a choice, or perhaps a collection of firm choices, that will produce the enduring growth you want and need. Growth is never automatic. It comes only because the two partners choose to make it the priority of their relationship.

Word on Today's Strength

Today's strength is not tomorrow's guarantee. What strength you have at this moment will not count much if you let it retreat tomorrow. Why do I make this statement? Because I have been watching more than a dozen Christian friends' marriages disintegrate. These were once good marriages in which the husband and wife refused to be set back by the problems and pressures of our times. But a false security had developed from their track records of fidelity and commitment. A track record isn't much good unless it is maintained.

Those of you who garden can identify with this illustration. When a plant is luxuriant and green, it is easy to give in to laziness and say, "It'll be all right today; I'll water it tomorrow instead." Sometimes that works. But not when the outside temperature holds at 103 degrees, as it is in the atmosphere surrounding our marriages. Normally plants don't brown and wither immediately. They can look good for days while the roots are drying out and becoming brittle.

We are prone to judge health by what we see above ground, and that can be terribly misleading. You certainly wouldn't want your physician to do that. As he does with his testing techniques and equipment to get to the root causes of our health problems, we must do with the marriages we treasure. But like plants, marriages can dry out until they're nearly impossible to revive . . . that is, from a human point of view. A marriage must be planted, nurtured, trimmed, and watched all the time—even daily—if it is going to thrive and flower for you.

The Scenario from Our Own Lives

In sharing our lives with you, Candee and I have had to take an in-depth look into the many rooms and closets of our relationship. We have even scoured the basement. It is like doing a good spring cleaning. We have observed how over time our strength has fluctuated and then increased.

We have learned, as close friends and lovers, that a one-time commitment by itself wasn't adequate to sustain a lifelong union. Our exchange of vows was merely the inauguration of our marriage.

On occasion, just like many of you, we have been so beleaguered by the process of growing together and accepting each other's challenging (often threatening) uniquenesses that we almost shelved our desire to have a great married life together. There were times when we saw little fulfillment of any kind. It seemed hopeless to continue.

However, we made it through those times and are today satisfied . . . deeply fulfilled.

In our eighteen years of marriage we have stumbled through a variety of tunnels that once seemed dark and endless. We entered marriage possessing strong, full-bodied personalities. And hitched to those strong personalities were trailers of strong opinions related to nearly everything and based on emotion instead of fact. These might not have been the problems they were to us at the time had it not been for our strong wills. And I mean strong!

For quite a while we were afraid of losing our identities to each other. As husband, I thought my leadership should be unchallenged, that my decisions should be made apart from Candee's input. When she was anxious to offer her thoughts, I felt that she was crowding my territory. As wife, Candee felt that God had brought her into the marriage to add a new dimension to her husband's life, but at the same time that marriage meant a shared attachment, not just a one-sided attachment. When I did not accept her thoughts and suggestions, it told her that a fundamental portion of who she was was being cast aside. The friction caused our identities to feel bruised and perhaps bound for extinction.

We did want to know a "one-flesh" relationship as the Bible terms it—a relationship where all of the both of us was totally joined together—but for some time we were not sure what that included. Most of our attempts at gaining it weren't too effective. Thus we frequently battled late into the night, even as we stayed true to our vows.

We also felt ripped off by misconceptions of marriage that were far removed from the truth. One of us had a "movie" view of romance. The other had simply misread the information that was available. Though the books we read tried to convey the reality that there would be conflict during a marriage's growth years, our lack of experience tended to filter away the information, leaving us a perspective that was overoptimistic, low on reality. We each tried to make our view the standard for our marriage.

Nonetheless, we tried to draw close to each other—on false premises—and we found the resulting disappointment crowded out our pleasure. Perhaps that's been your own experience.

Understanding the general roles of husband and wife was initially simple for us. It was the specifics inside those roles that gave us real difficulty. For example, did being a homemaker mean that Candee had to be strictly domestic? In other words, should the prevailing number of her interests, hobbies, and pursuits revolve around the home alone, or could some be aimed toward outside things as long as nothing at home which we had agreed upon was sacrificed?

I struggled with the same thing in my role as leader. What was I to do as head of the home, and how was I to carry it out? Actually, the tensions revolved more around style than around my duties. My tendency was to compare what I did with the way other seasoned pros were doing it in their homes. But in fact, the more I got to know those pros, the more I realized that behind the scenes they weren't the same as they appeared in the public's eye. As a couple, we won that battle when we decided for ourselves what the Neuenschwander home should be, irrespective of anyone else but God, and then stuck with the plan. The struggle subsided.

Though Candee and I had lots of common interests, we had many that weren't, and those aroused intermittent conflict and restlessness. For example, when we got time off we had two ideas of how we should spend it (and we still work on this today). One of us would want to accomplish projects. The other would want to relax and get away from it all. Even something as simple as turning on the car radio would tickle the problem. One of us would want to hear the news; the other preferred music, uninterrupted by the gore of the day's events.

Looking back, we can see that we felt hopeless on many occasions, even helpless to see any good change. And we had to come to terms with the changelessness of many situations we had not invited into our lives. In this kind of context we determined that we were going to grow and survive, even if we couldn't improve our circumstances. You know what we have learned? If you wait to grow until your circumstances are changed, you'll never grow.

Whether your marriage is healthy or in need of repair, I believe your journey through this book will help you take a fresh look at many of the dimensions of marriage. What I want you to see is that in spite of whatever history you and your mate have shared, with God's help and intervention you can preserve or recapture the friendship and romance you as individuals and a couple need to be satisfied on the earthside of life. Thank you for taking this journey with us.

Reflection

No marriage is problem free, for it cannot be any more perfect than the individuals who constitute it.

A growing marriage must operate on more than hope and intention alone. It must be undergirded by a carefully made choice to grow together.

The survival or death of your marriage will be determined by your ongoing choice to grow together.

Even the beleaguered and wounded have experienced the benign touch of God upon their lives and marriages.

Steps for Marital Growth

- ♥ What kinds of tough and feelingless choices have you made to protect your marriage?
- ♥ If it is unwise to judge the health of your marriage by what you see on the surface alone, then what should you look for that would give you a reliable pulse on your union?
- ♥ What things prevent you from making the positive choice of growing together in your marriage? What can you begin doing to make a difference?

2

Marriage:

The Shared Stroll of Two Living Souls

One sad tragedy of high-tech life is that few of us really take time to travel the steep, winding roads of our minds.

It seems that serious thinking is either time consuming or threatening to us. It's painful or problematic. And though we are capable of digging around and reasoning our way through a wide variety of significant issues, we tend to aim our thoughts toward those matters that lie just beyond the borders of our own beings: We focus on other people, on our jobs and hobbies, cars and houses, home computers, travel, politics and entertainment.

Sir John Davies understood the problem and described it this way:

> We that acquaint ourselves with every zone and pass both tropics and behold the poles, when we come home are to ourselves unknown, and unacquainted still with our own souls.
>
> Nosce Teipsum, 1599

Perhaps we could paraphrase his thought this way to better fit our own times: *We who familiarize ourselves with so many different kinds of learning and skill, and who travel from New York to Hawaii, from Israel to the Orient, when we come to necessary intermissions in our activities still have no idea who we really are.*

You see, when it comes to taking an inward look, we run or shrink back. We find that we are more fearful of knowing ourselves than of knowing others. And yet there is a growing hunger in our hearts to know ourselves and to be known by others. Many of you are searching to find yourselves, but you've been looking in all the wrong places.

In the past four months, three husbands I've known well have skipped home in a panic to find themselves. Lest you think that adultery was the principle cause for these separations, such was not the case. Though that's most often true, two of the three left because they were simply confused. They had lost their way, not even being sure any longer how to properly define that way.

For several years, each had gotten so caught up in the activities of parenting, earning an income, and keeping his possessions in good working order that he was basically moving from one crisis to another. They hadn't taken much time to be by themselves and think. They hadn't even spent times together with their wives doing the joint kind of thinking necessary to keep a marriage healthy. They were sprinting from this appointment to that seminar, and from this vocational challenge to that investment deal. Surprisingly, each man had plenty of relief time to be alone, but he used the time to play or work out—*religiously*! Playing they did . . . thinking they did not.

Then each on his own one day awoke only to realize he had no idea where he was going or why he was doing the things that occupied his appointment book. And as if overcome by a temporary insanity, each fled home, wife, and kids because he felt intensely confined. The men, like some of you, had paid little attention to the development of their minds and hearts, although each was sustaining most of the right activities all along. The result was that they'd evolved into well-dressed, "well- successed," and well-groomed machines going through the programming they had once given themselves, but no longer having any idea why.

When you no longer know yourself, the whys of life become obscure, even unimportant to you. When that happens to someone you've known and loved, it is shocking to observe. But when it is happening to you, you are the last to notice the change. And as with these men, the final stages of change strike fast and furiously, giving others the impression that the change occurred overnight.

Some of you are in the midst of such a change at this moment and need to come to terms with the problem before you get caught in its tight grip. None of us is immune to such a drift in our lives, and we must accept this reality and believe it can happen to us before we wake up one day to find ourselves broken individuals with broken relationships.

Recently I turned the final corner in a demanding grad school program. In the closing weeks, I had become so preoccupied with the demands imposed on me that I had little occasion to swim to the surface to catch life-giving breaths of fresh thought. I too had become a survivor, not a thinker. I was trying to make it from one day to the next without getting run down by those things I couldn't control. I was also striving to be a good parent to a teenager at one end of the quiver, and to a two-year-old at the other end, while keeping everyone else satisfied in between. Often I felt terribly fragmented.

Then, unexpectedly, God dropped a dear man into my life who had spent his career years in clinical and educational psychology. Having recently lost his son and in need of someone else who could share in his grief, he latched on to me and I to him. Through his own pain he came to know God intimately, and he began a reorganization of his own beliefs, which to that point had been primarily humanistic in nature.

Late one evening, while walking the streets of our neighborhood, Fraser turned and asked, "Who are you? How do you see yourself?" Confident that I had come to know myself quite well, I responded by giving him an answer describing my heart, goals, hopes, dreams, personality, character traits, activities, and achievements. I talked in terms of being a husband, father, friend, and counselor. When I finished, he said, "You've told me what you do and what you have done, but you haven't told me who you are. You really haven't answered my question." I suddenly felt awkward.

If that wasn't me that I had described, then who or what was the real Ed Neuenschwander?

Answering the Tough Question

Who am I? Awkward question, isn't it? All my years of education and training—church and otherwise—left me ill-prepared to answer it. It's not that I hadn't asked myself that before. In fact, questions of that sort had crawled into my thoughts periodically, but I didn't stick with the process of discovery long enough to find the right answers. On that particular evening a cherished friend helped me to sit patiently before an unsettling question until I could lock my thoughts in on an appropriate answer.

The Misguidance of Pop Psychology

The line I've heard so frequently from disoriented mates is:

> Because I do love my mate, I feel my leaving is best for them, as it is for me. Even the children will be happier because the atmosphere at home will be less tense. They'll adjust. We will all find a better life suited to our own needs.

However, from the sidelines I've watched these parting mates discover that the quality of happiness found in their subsequent relationships decries the value of this approach to solving the problem of husband-wife conflicts.

In my reading I've been drawn to the notions of Amitai Etzioni, a sociologist with his keen eye trained on our times. In his book, *An Immodest Agenda: Rebuilding America Before the Twenty-first Century*, he reveals his concern about the alarming trends he observes in our society. His conclusion is that America has experienced a hollowing in its fundamental social institutions because of self-oriented, self-focused concerns exhibited by mates, educators, neighbors, politicians, and others looking out for themselves.[1] This ego-centered mindset, he says, has been adopted by as much as eighty percent of our country's people and dangerously pushed along by the self-psychologies of our times.[2]

Of particular interest to me were his thoughts on pop psychology's "self-actualizing" approach to our development, which defeats rather than builds relationships. As I capsulize his thoughts for you, ask yourself, Does his conclusion address my attitude in my own marriage or in some other relationship I have?

Dr. Etzioni says that pop psychology directs a person to think about his or her own needs first, and it makes self-development and fulfillment the pinnacle of those needs. It sees affection and self-respect as "lower" needs, and it does not face the necessary balance between self-fulfillment and self-reality on the one hand, and affection and self-respect—the personal bases of mutuality—on the other.[3]

Different ones of you have entered therapy and found this to be the case for you. Instead of being helped to discover ways to rebuild your marriage (your original reason for seeking help), you have been encouraged to relocate and protect yourself. You also found yourself further from reconciliation than when you started.

Recently Marla, a middle-aged woman, introduced herself to me and told me how this had happened to her. She had come to the point of feeling out of place in her own marriage and had visited with an advisor who stressed that she had to discover "the real you." Her yearlong search led her into a dark alley where she felt more alone than before. She said, "It got to the point that no matter what my husband, Barry, did, he could not make

---

1. Amitai Etzioni, *An Immodest Agenda: Rebuilding America Before the Twenty-first Century* (New York: McGraw-Hill, 1983), pp. 95-96.

2. Ibid., pp. 39-42.

3. Ibid., p. 43.

progress with me. Why? Because my eye had become trained entirely upon myself."

When the conference drew to a close that weekend, she came to me and said with a gentle smile, "Barry didn't begin pulling away from me fifteen years ago. I pulled away from him, but I didn't realize it until yesterday." She went on to explain that the fulfillment of her needs, which had become the top priority for her "real me," had blocked any growth her marriage could have enjoyed. Her search for *me* sidetracked her original search for *us*.

Marla called me just recently to say, "Thanks again. We're continuing to grow as we focus our attention on each other." She sounded so settled and at home in her rediscovered relationship with Barry. Exciting, isn't it? It almost gives you hope for your own struggles, doesn't it?

It is important to know who we are and to be fulfilled. But the answer to the question Who am I? cannot be found through self-inquiry alone. We must turn to God for the answer. We cannot search for ourselves apart from his ideals, nor can we locate our true selves apart from our marriages and mates. We must first begin our search by looking at ourselves as our Designer sees us. Then we must adjust our perceptions and relationships to suit that discovery.

The Trustworthy Guidance of Scripture

Thanks to the Bible, we can make our way back to the thoughts and feelings of God. By asking Who am I? and Who are you? while consulting its pages, we can locate the answer that will give new life to any relationship we have, regardless of the level it's on. The counsel of the Old Testament takes us all back to our original design, back to the basic model of humankind. If we believe and accept the information without adding to it, then we will see one another in purest form. It's there that a meaningful, growing marriage must begin.

This question, which has gained contemporary prominence, was asked by one hero of the faith back in the tenth century B.C. Standing on a Jerusalem rooftop, or perhaps on a deserted Palestinian slope, David listened in his inner person to the message projected by the starlit heavens above him which spoke of God and his creative deeds. Many of you can appreciate David's discovery because the best times you have alone in your thoughts come when you sit patiently under a star-studded sky, looking up and allowing God to orchestrate your meditation.

As David pondered the heavens, he wrote these words, addressing the Lord's splendor and man's dignity. As you read them, look beyond their poetical structure and listen to the inquiring heart of an ancient husband and dad. Notice how he handles the question, Who (or what) is man?

> When I consider Thy heavens, the work of Thy fingers,
> The moon and the stars, which Thou hast ordained;
> *What is man,* that Thou dost take thought of him?
> . . . Yet Thou hast made him a little lower than God,
> And dost crown him with glory and majesty!
> Thou dost make him to rule over the works of Thy hands; Thou hast put all things under his feet.
>
> Psalm 8:3-6 (emphasis added).

Why? What is it about man that God considered him worthy to be crowned with a special glory and majesty? The answer is found in two statements made by the author of Genesis. First, we read in Genesis 2:7:

> The LORD God formed man of dust from the ground, and breathed into his nostrils the breath of life; and man became a living being.

And second, going back yet closer to the opening words of Scripture, Genesis 1:26-27 tells us:

> Then God said, "Let Us make man in Our image, according to Our likeness; and let them rule. . . ." And God created man in His own image, in the image of God He created him; male and female He created them.

Though it is hard for us to grasp, we possess this conferred glory and majesty and hold a preeminent place in God's created order because God made us to be a likeness and image of himself. And different from any other created entity, you contain something which God took from himself and placed, or breathed, into you.

Perhaps it will help you to know that the term *being* was taken originally from the word *to breathe* and has been rendered in various biblical texts as "soul," "life," and "breath." Take a moment and think through the connection.

In practical terms, this means each of us is a living breath that is God-breathed (that includes your mate and your kids). Miss this point and you'll miss the most important basis of any human relationship—your marriage or otherwise.

The wonderful mystery of life is that God breathed something of his being into our lungs. He gave us the very principle of life itself. God's life-giving breath gave our sculpted dust its animation; it inaugurated the human soul and personality; and it caused functions to begin that spoke of design and purpose and resulted in usefulness, reward, and pleasure. The hard reality for us to face is that without God's breath, we would fall to the ground and lose our identities to the soil. Coming to terms with this will produce the genuine humility in us which is so urgently needed in all of our relationships.

What a Fresh View Can Do for Us

What does all this mean? What can and should be the impact upon our earthbound mindsets? I have at least three suggestions to offer you which may cause a whole new era of relationship to be born in your marriage. Each is expressed with the words of David from Psalm 8:5 in mind. The first is this:

> Recognizing each other as living souls "crowned with glory and majesty" causes us to think differently about the ways we treat each other.

As Candee and I reflected on this life-changing principle, we realized it called for some sharp changes in our behavior. We needed to rethink the ways we talked to each other, the ways we expressed our humor, the ways we kept our promises, the ways we prayed for and supported each other. To restate this principle, *the manner by which you care for your mate is the most important demonstration to God of how you feel toward him.*

Got that? The manner in which you treat each other is the paramount statement you make to God about how you feel toward him.

Surprisingly, evangelism isn't the most important thing you offer to God. Nor is the worship you offer in a service. Neither is the giving of your possessions to make possible the continuance of a church ministry in this desperate age of ours.

The way you treat your husband, your wife, and others both in public and private is the most demonstrative declaration you can make to God. Why? Because something vital of himself has been implanted in the person to whom you are related.

What's my support for such a conclusion? you may ask. It is Jesus' own statement, found in Matthew 25:34-40. Though the specific context of his address is a future judgment, the principle he presents has broader application that seeps right into our personal lives today.

> Then the King [referring to himself] will say to those on His right, "Come, you who are blessed of My Father, inherit the kingdom prepared for you from the foundation of the world. For I was hungry, and you gave Me something to eat; I was thirsty, and you gave Me drink; I was a stranger, and you invited Me in; naked, and you clothed Me; I was sick, and you visited Me; I was in prison, and you came to Me."
>
> Then the righteous will answer Him, saying, "Lord, when did we see You hungry, and feed You, or thirsty, and give you drink? And when did we see You a stranger, and invite You in, or naked, and clothe You? And when did we see You sick, or in prison, and come to You?"
>
> And the King will answer and say to them, "*Truly I say to you, to the extent that you did it to one of these brothers of Mine, even the least of them, you did it to Me*" (emphasis added).

You know what we noticed, even in our own relationship as a husband and wife? Sometimes the stranger got the preferred, more gentle treatment over the mate or over the child. We don't like that in us, so we work all the time to correct that tendency in our marriage.

Our second principle is:

> Recognizing each other as living souls "crowned with glory and majesty" gives new understanding to the nature and motivation of commitment.

Why is that so? Because with the realization of who you both are, there comes the accompanying sense that when you walk out on each other, you walk out on God as well. You can go through all the right religious exercises and carry on all the right spiritual activities, but they add up to very little when you've pulled away from your mate. We are not saying that salvation is lost or forfeited, but something very fundamental to your fellowship with God is injured when you pull up roots and part company.

In our present culture, Christian and otherwise, commitment is endorsed until it brings discomfort or until work has to be done to preserve the relationship. If we can't be happy, then we discount commitment's binding nature. Through the pen of Solomon, God gives us his point of view on this life matter. It's to be taken seriously.

> When you make a vow to God, do not be late in paying it, for He takes no delight in fools. Pay what you vow! It is better that you should not vow than that you should vow and not pay. Do not let your speech cause you to sin and do not say in the presence of the messenger of God that it was a mistake. Why should God be angry on account of your voice and destroy the work of your hands? (Ecclesiastes 5:4- 6).

You see, God is anxious to protect and preserve the feelings and futures of his living souls, much as we might struggle with that thought at times. And whether it is a promise you make to a person about money or marriage or relationships, you've got to think again before breaking it. Vows are binding from God's point of view.

The third principle from Psalm 8:5 is:

> Recognizing each other as living souls "crowned with glory and majesty" leads to the restoration of the preferred treatment once shown each other in the earliest days of the romance.

A beloved friend of mine who was a military officer, now retired, tells the most wonderful story of how his relationship to his wife came alive thirteen years ago when he realized this very thing. Let me pass his story on to you.

Jack had negotiated his way through life like most people. In the military he moved up the career path, inheriting greater responsibility. He had lived with his own set of struggles which beset him along the way, keeping in check his ability to have the most fulfilling marriage.

Ellen, his wife, hungering for something more, fell into a caring group of Christian women studying Scripture and allowing it to remodel their desires and attitudes. Ellen in time discovered Christ and learned how he could reach into her and bring about the fundamental changes she desired.

In time Jack, wanting something more himself, began attending a Bible study to understand what had happened to his wife of twenty years. Eventually it became clear to him what had transpired in Ellen's life. And Jack, as awkward as he felt about it, asked Christ to be his Savior. Within a year their courtship had begun to grow and is still growing. In fact, Jack and Ellen's romance has come into full bloom and its fragrance is enjoyed by those surrounding them. As Jack began seeing Ellen as one whom God saw as glorious and majestic, he began showing her the touches of love he first felt as a young, unseasoned lover.

Making a Turn-Around

For those of you who have been mismanaging your relationships and wish to experience healing in your homes, or those who have had a relatively good marriage, yet sense it could become more intimate, here are several steps you may implement to turn yourself around.

1. Acknowledge before God that you are a living soul who is God-breathed. Then make that same acknowledgment regarding your mate.

2. Accept your husband or wife as a full-bodied, full-souled expression of God himself.

3. Aim your eye toward seeing the bedrock beauty in the heart of your soul-mate.

4. Adjust your priorities in order to have the time you need to nurture, protect, and preserve your mate's life just as you would your own.

When you better understand yourself and your mate through God's eyes, your feelings for each other deepen. But when you don't acquire perspective of this sort, you carry confusion into your marriage at ground level. Without this outlook, your romance can only be fragile, and its permanence will be threatened.

Reflection

You are not simply living with a mate, but with a God-breathed living soul.

As you begin caring properly for that living soul, your regard for him will change.

The resulting change in perspective will give birth to a much-needed sense of warmth and security.

That warmth and security will establish an atmosphere for renewed friendship and love.

And the pleasure of renewed friendship will clear the passage for an authentic and gratifying romance.

Steps for Marital Growth

- ♥ Stop to consider that you possess something of God himself within you. How does thinking this enhance your own worth? How does this affect your view of your mate?

- ♥ The way you treat your mate, handle his emotions, and pay attention to his growth and development makes the greatest statement to God about how you really feel toward him. How does this differ from the attitude you've had up until now?
- ♥ Turn to Psalm 8:3-6 and personalize its thoughts. Speak or write down the words as though they came from you. Thinking of you or thinking of your mate, what questions surface and what conclusions do you draw?
- ♥ Think of some changes you could make in your marriage that would express to your mate the preferred treatment he deserves—in spite of the rough edges or the pain and injury he has brought to you in the past.

3

Romance:

The Heart of Marriage

We're not strangers to illusions. In fact, every time we have been betrayed by one, we've been disappointed and often embarrassed because of our gullibility. While many illusions are obvious, others are not. Here are some of the more familiar illusions we've courted at one time or another:

- Life will be adventuresome and wonderful, without the invasion of surprise, disaster, or death.
- Parenting will be secure and sensational, without the intrusion of distance or rebellion.
- Marriage will be blissful and smooth, without the entrance of conflict, heartache, or misunderstanding.
- Investing will be successful and safe, without the occurrence of loss or reverse.
- Vacations will be quiet and restful, without the interference of accident or theft.
- Romance will be intense and endless, without the impediment of adjustment, boredom, or change.

We all have stories to tell of illusions which have been rudely overthrown by reality . . . some funny, others painful. And most of us know too well the lyrics that rise up from the smoldering rubble of our destroyed illusions: "Give up; you can't win; there's little hope for something better." Those lines are intimidating. They can easily override God's offer of hope for our lives.

Scott Peck, writing as a contemporary observer and not as a theologian, describes one illusion that's had serious impact on many marital romances. In his book entitled *The Road Less Traveled*, he writes:

> To serve as effectively as it does to trap us into marriage, the experience of falling in love probably must have as one of its characteristics the illusion that the experience will last forever. . . . The myth of romantic loves tells us, in effect, that for every young man in the world there is a young woman who was "meant for him," and vice versa. Moreover, the myth implies that there is only one man meant for a woman and only one woman for a man and this has been predetermined "in the stars." When we meet the person for whom we are intended, recognition comes through the fact that we fall in love. We have met the person for whom all the heavens intended us, and since the match is perfect, we will then be able to satisfy all of each other's needs forever and ever, and therefore live happily forever after in perfect union and harmony. Should it come to pass, however, that we do not satisfy or meet all each other's needs and friction arises and we fall out of love, then it is clear that a dreadful mistake was made, we misread the stars, we did not hook up with our one and only perfect match, what we thought was love was not real or "true" love, and nothing can be done about the situation except to live unhappily ever after or get divorced.[1]

He adds, "Millions of people waste vast amounts of energy desperately and futilely attempting to make the reality of their

1. M. Scott Peck, *The Road Less Traveled* (New York: Simon and Schuster, 1978), p. 91.

lives conform to the unreality of the myth."[2] Those of the Christian community are not often different. They too are numbed by this myth.

Many of us are still trying to cling to illusions and myths about romance that corrupt rather than clarify our marriage relationships. In the pages that follow, I'd like to shatter the myth and rebuild a biblically sound platform upon which to reconstruct our hopes and dreams.

Where Romance Fits In

By our society's standard, romance is central to life. This is often exemplified in the workaday world where the pursuit of romance often gets in the way of many a man's or woman's professional responsibilities. Their passions become overpowering, since their thoughts are camped on the crest of their perceived romantic needs. Then when they meet someone both attractive and vulnerable to them, their good judgment becomes scrambled, their erotic urges take charge, and their responsibilities are surrendered to the moment. The business community often fosters this.

John, my valued friend who is a successful, God-honoring businessman, recently told me that his fellow executives were trying to sell him on the rewards of divorce. Each associate had already divorced his wife in order to enjoy the acclaimed sexual freedoms available to him in their line of work. Like so many of you, John stands alone among his peers. Why? He wants an enduring romance, but he wants the one which he began with his wife nearly twenty years ago. He figures that if he can't make it work with Bev it probably won't work with anyone else. Any other romance would leave him nothing but emptiness, guilt, and sorrow. And he knows! He has seen it lived out in the lives of his colleagues.

Incidentally, each of John's co-workers has confused love, romance, and sexual freedom with one another. As so many people do, they use the terms synonymously.

2. Ibid., p. 92.

Romance Clarified

The term *romance* gives us lots of trouble. Ask married people what it is they are seeking and their answers vary drastically. Too often mates themselves adopt differing definitions. It's no wonder their needs go unfulfilled in this respect. They are each in pursuit of something different, though they give it the same label, and they believe the other to be in search of the same experience when in reality he's not.

As words, *love*, *romance*, and *sex* are used frequently by people in search of some fulfillment in life they haven't been able to clarify themselves. The confusion is no better seen than in the thinking of our children. I asked Heather, my fourteen-year-old, to define romance from the thoughts she'd collected from her peers. My daughter answered with these words: "Romance is a physical and emotional attraction between two people that can't be helped." Physical . . . emotional attraction. There it is!

That's the troublesome thread spliced into our thinking and into our relationships. Perhaps the way many of us have managed our romances has even helped to underscore that conclusion in our children's thinking. We've given credibility to the false statements made by the musicians and artists of our times, who seem to set the pace for us.

As we begin to challenge our assumptions, let's ask: What about those who've been left with physical limitations from birth or accident? Is romance beyond their reach? If they cannot function sexually, are they deprived of romantic feelings and expressions? What about those whose bodies have been ravaged by disease? Is romance off-limits to them? Are their eyes no longer allowed to grow misty because of the thoughts and warmth they feel as their souls interlock with each other?

We need to keep these and similar questions in mind as we proceed. They help us to shatter the myth that romantic love is related only to physical or erotic love. Let's agree now that romance may include sexual expression, but romance and sex are not synonymous.

Needed: A No-Nonsense Approach to Romance

Most of what we think about today in terms of romance seems to deal with cosmetic realities. I think of men like Bob and Scott as I say this. Each is in his forties. One is a self-employed construction worker. The other is a business administrator. But they both perform as though they were reading the same script. When each thinks of being romantic he does so in terms of creating a romantic mood, finding a romantic environment, or taking his wife to a romantic play, concert, or restaurant. When they want to be super-romantic, they throw in a limousine service.

As a side note, the truth is that many mates find the idea of being romantic and in love better than its reality. They find the setting of romance more pleasurable than the person who's by their side or sitting across the table from them.

In both these relationships the wives have reacted the same, even though they've never met one another. Usually when Linda and Marilyn discover such a "romantic" evening in the making, they sense there's a hidden agenda: intercourse. And what should have been surprising and exciting becomes disgusting because of one thing: The interludes between such events were not characterized by concern, care, gentleness, thoughtfulness, love, and focused attention. Bob and Scott have yet to learn that.

These men, like so many of us, need to ask, Does the setting make the person, or does the person make the setting? Are the interludes important, and can the main events be meaningful apart from them?

Both the setting and the individual are important, but only the person is essential. The setting is incidental. And it's the way we treat the interludes that makes the greatest statements of how we think and feel about romance. Many husbands and wives have failed because they have shown more respect for settings and environments than for that which counts the most: the ongoing communion and interchange of their souls . . . day after day!

Here's what happens: When we have neglected the interludes, we tend to choose settings that take our attention off each other, places where our gaze is arrested by noise and motion. And we do this because the time leading up to that magic moment has been neither magic nor pleasant. We've been too busy, too cranky, too selfish, too demanding. Thus we let sensational settings be substitutes for an affectionate gaze and a moving and growing soul relationship. We place the heaviest emphasis on the romantic evening in order to again become short-term friends and lovers. In this way we unwittingly widen the gap between our souls.

This is not to say that romantic moods, places, and events are unimportant. They are important. They're both necessary and desirable. But they are only meaningful if we have been truly romantic with one another apart from these things. In other words, *romantic appointments cannot be substitutes for regularly expressed, genuine, mature romantic actions.*

God's Thoughts on Romance

In no other relationship but marriage is so much of ourselves involved. In no other relationship are so many different aspects of ourselves expressed. Because this is so, and if we are to move from myth to reality, we need to look through a scriptural window to see into God's mind on this matter.

Though the term *romance* does not appear in the Bible, the concept does. When we think of romance, we would do ourselves a great favor to think of "an intimate communion shared by soulmates."

Let's go back to the roots of the man-woman relationship found in Genesis 2 and view it through God's eyes. The biblical record describes how God, after forming man, placed him in the garden to cultivate and keep it (v. 15). Then he said, "It is not good for the man to be alone; I will make him a helper suitable for him" (v. 18). The term *alone* has the connotation of "acute loneliness and emptiness." God, in looking at his created man, recognized that he had a hole in his heart; and although it was within God's power to plug it with himself alone, he chose instead to create another human being to occupy that emotional (not spiritual) void. He decided to create a corresponder, someone "suitable for him" (v. 18). The word *suitable* is critically important to us who want a lasting romance, for it holds our key to understanding; it means "to place something high, to make it conspicuous." The idea is that God made a complement for Adam who would totally seize his attention . . . one who would become the central object of his focus.

I hope you don't miss this clue to a healthy relationship. We could so easily jog past this observation and miss the whole point of marriage. You see, Adam had not yet sinned when God observed his need. God was not displeased when he recognized Adam's longing for something or someone else. He didn't even reprove the man for feeling acutely lonely. Instead, from a heart of love, God made another person for Adam—alike in nature—to eradicate his loneliness. Simply put, before Eve's entry into his life, Adam was incomplete emotionally and psychologically.

When God finished his work of making the woman, Adam gave a reaction worth noting: "This is now bone of my bones, and flesh of my flesh" (v. 23). Observe first that he was excited, and second that he was satisfied. He felt whole. At last he was complete. He had someone who was his very own: one with whom he could share and live life; one with whom he could eat, work, laugh, cry, play, and sleep; one who could touch him when he was discouraged and weary, and whom he could himself touch in the same way and to the same extent.

The text continues: "For this cause a man shall leave his father and his mother, and shall cleave to his wife; and they shall become one flesh" (v. 24). Within this verse there is another clue that solves a relationship-inspiring mystery. It's contained in the word *flesh*. John N. Oswalt, a keen student of the Old Testament, tells us how the terms *flesh* (or *body*) and *soul* were often used in parallel fashion within the Scriptures. With that in mind, note closely what he says:

> To refer to someone as being one's own "flesh and bone" (Genesis 2:23) was to say more than that they shared the same bodily heritage. Again, to say that a

> man and woman become one flesh in the sexual embrace (Genesis 2:24) is to say more than that they are united bodily.[3]

Becoming one flesh embodies the whole of genuine romance in marriage. That is, *romance is the collective process of growing to fully know and accept one another . . . of being soul-mated.*

In our marriage, Candee and I have come to think of romance as the mental, emotional, and physical communion we constantly share with each other. And with God's help we have become students of one another, seeking to know thoroughly all aspects of the other's life. We are learning to ask each other better questions. We are taking time to observe each other in all kinds of settings. We are working to find the balance between listening and sharing. We want to fully know each other's souls.

Putting it all together, we could say that romance is a mental, emotional, and physical communion two people in love share which may be enhanced by "romantic" moods and settings and touches. But romance is not a setting. It is the relationship we have as soul-mates which can be taken into and out of a wide variety of settings—"romantic" ones included!

Recurring Tragedies

When love and romance are not maturely rooted in soul-to-soul involvement, then a variety of tragedies develop. Here are some common examples:

Choosing substitutes. Instead of focusing attention on each other and the development of their relationships, many couples have allowed surrogates to take over, surrogates such as sports, educational programs, community or church involvements, hobbies, adjunct friendships, employment, even children or parents.

Jean and Frank did just this. Some time back Jean developed a deep concern for women who seemed confused about

---

3. R. Laird Harris, et al., *The Theological Wordbook of the Old Testament* (Chicago: Moody Press, 1980), p. 136.

life. She felt that if she could help them better understand God through Bible study, then she could help bring about change in her world. She and Frank had a mediocre marriage, and it wasn't long before she found herself absorbed around the clock with this activity that brought her such great fulfillment. This good thing in her life actually prevented her from giving attention to the improvement of her own marriage. While many sang her praises, her husband felt orphaned.

In time Frank, who became crowded out of her life, gave up and courted his business with the same fervor with which Jean nurtured her Bible study ministry. He lost his zeal for deepening their relationship while she felt continually stroked by those she served. Today they remain together as house tenants, but their hearts are worlds apart.

Jean's story is all too familiar. Many times in recent years I have observed couples—both lay and professional—who've allowed ministry activity within their church or parish or within some other people-oriented agency to become the substitute that has hurt, rather than helped their relationships.

When a relationship is sacrificed for ministry (or any other noble cause), a double tragedy occurs. Not only is the union destroyed, but so is the message regarding Christ and his ability to bring life and hope to ailing couples. *None of us can be responsible people and at the same time allow career, ministry, play, or anything else to become the all-consuming diet of our lives.*

Losing the original dream. The exchange of vows was designed by God to be a safeguard to a marriage, to protect the sacred husband-wife relationship, to preserve a romantic friendship. Its purpose was not to bring about its death. But all too frequently, romance begins to die at the altar. Then within months, as marital adjustment picks up steam, the relationship begins to cough chronically. Why? Perhaps it's because the soul mates have lost sight of a fundamental issue.

My friend and former colleague Dr. Cyril Barber and I were talking one day about reasons some marriages disintegrate. What he said made sense: "In biblical times people married in order to love, but today we seem to love only in order to marry." I believe for many that is true. Lots have forgotten the original dream: We married in order to continue our love affair. The wedding ceremony is not to be the climax of a union. Instead, it is supposed to be the transaction that gives permanence to a romance and a well-fenced refuge to a shared struggle of two lives.

Jim and Brenda lost the original dream. Here's how it happened. In love's first days, the initial attraction of their two souls was soon overcome by intense and surging emotions which to them were pleasurable. Their loneliness fled. The aching vacuums in their merging souls were temporarily soothed by the mutual touching of their lives. They experienced excitement, security, and a newfound purpose for living. Life went from black and white to full-orbed color. Their love was overtaken by a heartthrob which veterans of good marriages have realized cannot endure indefinitely.

When the intensity of falling in love subsided, they interpreted it to be an undeniable symptom telling them their love was in trouble. Doubt set in, and they began saying to themselves, "Our love has died an untimely death."

Like Jim and Brenda, some of you have been repeating the same line. In fact, there are those who cannot tear themselves away from this false conclusion, so they have given up because they can't resuscitate their lifeless feelings. They ask counselors to help them recapture what's been lost. They have developed a fixation on their lost emotional state. And instead of waking up to the serious side of the commitment they made that could keep the original dream alive, they have redoubled their efforts to search for the relationship of their dreams and faulty past fantasies.

Tragically, the Jims and Brendas of this world are oblivious to the fact that immature, idealistic romance must recede and die if mature romance is going to rise in its place. This is the only way couples can find the soul-satisfaction they both so desperately need.

Sexual intimacy without romance. Another recurring tragedy is reflected in the complaint of many wives who feel their husbands do not—or cannot—make a distinction between sex and romance.

Dr. Ed Wheat, in his invaluable book entitled *Love Life*, describes the necessity of romantic physical touching apart from sex. He writes:

> Touching is the most natural act in the world, and our need for it is more basic than our need for sex. Sex falls into the category of desire, for unmarried people can live happy, fulfilled lives without it. But the caring touch of another human being is a need that should not be ignored. At birth, touch was our first line of communication. The cuddling and loving we received was necessary for our emotional development, even for our physical well-being. Now that we are adults, very little has changed. We still have a deep need for the warmth, reassurance, and intimacy of non-sexual touching whether we are conscious of it or not. Often we turn to sex when what we really want is the comfort of loving closeness. . . . Psychologists believe that American preoccupation with sex these days is really a longing for the emotionally supportive physical affection that every human craves, but which has been in short supply in our culture.[4]

Not long ago, I was with a group of couples at a weekend retreat. While meeting with the men who were interested in learning how to better love their wives, I decided to ask them a series of questions based upon increasing complaints I'd been hearing from wives. Were their wives correct in their gripes? I was curious to know. Here are two of the questions I asked the men:

1. When was the last time you spent a memorable day or evening with your wife without expecting to end it with sex?
2. How often have you touched your wife this month apart from any occasion of intercourse?

Each of the men was asked to evaluate himself in silence, and as they did so, they could be heard chuckling or groaning in pain. None dared nudge another; reality was too severe. A

4. Ed Wheat, *Love Life for Every Married Couple* (Grand Rapids: Zondervan, 1980), p. 136.

physician approached me afterward to show me his evaluation, and true to character he had given himself letter grades. To each of these questions he had honestly given himself a D minus while wondering if he really didn't deserve an F. (His wife would have agreed with the latter, based on what she'd told me.) The others tested out just about as poorly as he did. However, he went home with a renewed intention to push his performance to the top end of the scale. Guess what? He's succeeding!

Giving up prematurely. When romance appears to be diminishing, often pessimism moves in. We tend to think we cannot recapture romance. Every day couples are parting because they're convinced that any effort to re-establish their dwindling romance is merely contrived or mechanical. The pain of divorce seems to be easier to handle than the misery of their lifeless love affairs.

Apart from God's intervention, perhaps that's the most likely conclusion to reach. But too many husbands and wives who were once enemies have discovered God's remarkable ability to touch their deceased romances and call them back to life. He's given good health to their marriages and friendships, reconciling their severe differences so they could again freely love each other . . . or possibly even love each other for the first time.

The problem isn't with God or his ability to invade our bedrooms and living space. The problem is with us who quit before he's been given the opportunity to turn trouble into testimony.

It's time for us to look away from the problem and examine the solution. The question is this: If we're having difficulty, is there something we can do to put our romance back together? The good news is "yes!"

How to Revive or Enhance Your Romance

Recently, Candee and I visited with several couples who were discussing the subjects of love and romance. Amy asked, "How can you go back and rekindle the feeling you had in the beginning of your relationship?" As the others of us listened with interest, she went on to describe how activities and demands related to business, children, parents, and other things had dried up "the feelings of romance" she had once enjoyed for Don.

As the discussion continued, it became apparent to all of us that you cannot go back and recapture the feelings of the past. Instead, you have to pick up where you are now . . . today . . . and nurture your relationship amid the demands which your lives have accumulated and that you cannot shed.

Mature romantic love, carefully nurtured, inspires, enriches, motivates, energizes, and renews. But it does not develop automatically. It grows in time as we make and trade romantic expressions and actions. Romantic actions breed romantic feelings. Exercise must precede emotion. But we must keep in mind that the feelings which will emerge will be new ones, not merely revived old feelings that we still have pegged to the walls of our memories.

I would like to suggest to you a handful of activities that Candee and I have found effective for building a biblically sound romance. Why not give them a try in your own marriage?

First, *determine to give your relationship first position in your scheme of things* (assuming, of course, that your relationship with God is what it should be).

Second, *readjust your priorities and activities so that you can gain the time needed to fully know and accept one another.*

Third, *develop your senses of romance.* Specifically:

- With your eyes, study your mate. Observe him or her as he sleeps, as he works, as he relates to your children and friends, as he expresses himself in his own comfortable settings.
- With your ears, try to hear the things he is working to tell you which reveal his deepest feelings of joy, excitement, hurt, and desire.
- With your heart, provide him an entrance so that he may come into your life in order to fully take up residence. Put yourself on display. Try to say what you feel (though it may be awkward to do so).

Fourth, *practice asking questions that create opportunities to discuss the day, the past, their thoughts and wishes about the future—its hopes and hitches.*

Fifth, *be creative in your expressions of love and interest.* Now and then, opt for a surprise—whether it's an expression, a gift, or a getaway. Be courageous and step beyond your normal ruts. Keep it fresh.

Sixth, *show unsolicited acts of love and thoughtfulness*—hugs, kisses, and the touches of a loving heart.

All of these must emerge in the right kind of climate. Dr. Wheat's counsel is so good . . . and wise! He says:

> In providing the right emotional climate, do all you can to avoid boredom even though your life must of necessity consist of routine. Think of your relationship as a continuing love affair and look at every tender, generous, romantic word or act that you bestow on your partner as an investment in pleasurable memories and emotional experiences that can grow and multiply into romantic love.[5]

Reflection

The search for romance has led many couples into a loveless desert where only mirages of love and romance exist, created by the writers and artists of current and past times.

Romantic ideals, moods, places, and events, though they might be important, cannot be substituted for sincere and purposed romantic actions of the heart.

In no other relationship but marriage is so much of ourselves involved and made vulnerable. Thus if we are to find refuge and move from myth to reality, we need to adopt a pattern of romance that's honored both by Scripture and time.

When God placed man and woman into marriage, it was his desire for them to become the focused objects of each others' attention. In view of this, an enduring view of romance must include the collective process of growing to fully know and accept one another . . . of being soul-mated.

5. Ibid., p. 91.

Since authentic romance must be based upon realism, at some point idealistic romance will have to recede and die if mature romance is going to sprout up in its place.

Many who have watched the romance which they carried into marriage die have seen God resurrect their love affairs and give them both new hope and a new attraction. They have seen him breathe new life into a once-fragile union. Those who thought they'd never again know romance have gained one that is more compelling than before . . . and durable, at that!

Steps for Marital Growth

- How do you define romance? How do your thoughts differ from those of your mate? Have the differences in thinking put stress on your relationship? If so, how?
- If you were to compare love, sex, and romance, how would each differ from the other? Where would they overlap?
- Turn to 1 Corinthians 13:4-8 and review Paul's counsel regarding love. Love is the fuel that keeps romance alive and growing. A rethinking of romance is faulty if you fail to reassess your thinking about love. Spend some time measuring the quality of your own love by the characteristics he describes in the text.

4

Friendship:

The Heart of Romance

In his work entitled *Love's Comedy II*, Henrik Ibsen commented, "A friend married is a friend lost." Perhaps that observation best depicts one of the prevailing tragedies of modern romance. It is my firm belief that whereas mature romance is the heart of marriage, *friendship is the heart of romance.* When friendship is missing, so is the catalyst for a growing romance.

I find pleasure in meeting seasoned couples who have learned the art of keeping their friendships alive and growing. You see, friendship helps a marriage move more comfortably through life's more painful seasons; it injects zest and vitality into a relationship, causing it to rise beyond the level of mere coexistence. In a practical (and not theological) sense, what reason is there for marriage if friendship is of little concern to those involved?

Most every couple I've observed began their marriage thinking the exchange of vows would both enhance and secure the friendship they'd come to treasure. Maybe that was your thinking; certainly it was mine. Candee and I met in the summer of

1966 and immediately found ourselves in the most challenging and satisfying friendship we had ever known. By midsummer we were engaged and anxious to marry. Five months later we married with the intention of being together all the time so our friendship could continue to grow without the hindrances of separate residences and long-distance driving.

Like many of you, we soon discovered that marriage didn't necessarily make the friendship easier to preserve. Actually, we found it became more complicated, primarily because many new stress-producing factors were introduced into the relationship. Immediately we had to learn how to survive each other's differences in living patterns, standards of order and neatness, approaches to cooking and washing dishes. Added to these were the complicated matters of sexual and emotional adjustment. We weren't totally prepared for the reality that crouched behind the fantasy of our wonderful courtship.

We quickly found it took work to pull off a friendship between a husband and wife. And we began to learn that friendship does not grow apart from cultivation.

Mates can't cultivate a friendship if they don't recall what a friend is. What is a friend? Simply put, *a friend is one who knows you well and is still fond of you . . . one from whom you receive and to whom you give love, support, and empathy.* A friend has been described as *one who stands on the same side of the struggle with you.* Some insightful observer has said, "A true friend will see you through when others see that you are through." That's just what Candee does for me. That's what I try to do for her.

Before going on, pause a moment and ask yourself, Am I that kind of person? Does my mate see me in those terms? Don't think about your marriage partner at this point. Focus attention on yourself. Friendship propagates friendship. If you initiate friendship with your husband or wife, most likely in time they will reciprocate.

The Hallmarks of Authentic Friendship

In Scripture, I find at least three qualities of friendship that should be a part of marital relationship. Candee and I have purposed to make them part of the bond we share. As you think about each one, ask God to show you which ones you and your mate need to revive or cultivate.

Oneness . . . "Who is as your own soul." A brief description of a friend surfaces in a most unexpected spot in the Old Testament: amid a warning against idolatry. In naming specific people who could detour one's loyalty to God, Moses called attention to "your friend who is as your own soul" (Deuteronomy 13:6). Don't hurry past that phrase. It holds an important clue to friendship.

Moses wasn't the only one to think of a friend in these terms. So did John Lyly in his work entitled *Euphenes*. Here's how he put it:

> A friend is in prosperity a pleasure, a solace in austerity, in grief a comfort, in joy a merry companion, and at all times another I.

Although separated by thousands of years, both men recognized that in a close relationship it's hard to determine where one person ends and the other begins. Those who have cultivated friendship in marriage have especially found this to be true. Candee and I have discovered that as our hearts have become more tightly bonded, an immeasurable overlap of emotions and thoughts, ideals and dreams have resulted.

Most couples have experienced oneness of this sort to some extent in their earliest days together, first during courtship, then after their vows were exchanged, and as their new home was being established. In fact, my counseling of couples in crisis has shown me that most people originally married to sustain the very friendship that prompted their romances.

Isn't it strange how something we initially feel so protective of slips through the cracks as time passes? Some lose this emotional oneness too quickly because they think that physical oneness is the answer to all their needs for intimacy. This is particularly true for those in their early years of wedlock.

Here are four reasons Candee and I have identified which threaten emotional oneness:

- Our false expectations we carry into marriage fall apart, and disillusionment soon sets in.
- The various adjustments we encounter take us by surprise, so we tend to withdraw from each other to avoid further pain.
- When our eyes begin to see the real person we married (as opposed to the person we knew during courtship), we start to feel like a stranger in our home. Commitment begins to press on us.
- The rapidly emerging differences in our personalities and dispositions and viewpoints seem threatening; thus we become increasingly self-protective.

Each of us has to aggressively fight such intruders as soon as they first appear on the thresholds of our relationships. If we don't, they will undermine our ability to share in the experience of being one soul.

Durability . . . "Loves at all times." Another quality of friendship that should be found in marriage is that friendship is held together by enduring love—love that does not fatigue prematurely. From Solomon's pen comes this statement: "A friend loves at all times, and a brother is born for adversity" (Proverbs 17:17). The context of this particular proverb is harsh times. Keep that in mind as we think for a moment about his sage counsel.

On the surface, the term *all* seems innocuous, but in reality, it is so troublesome for most of us. Loving "at all times" is tough work, if not impossible; yet it stands as an unmistakable characteristic of true friendship. Honestly, aren't we more comfortable with exception words like *mostly, intermittently,* and *frequently?* They seem to fit better with our fallen natures. They don't ask so much of us. Though we prefer them, they don't find their way into Solomon's vocabulary. And the fact is, we are expected by God, even as married friends, to love at all times.

How many times have you watched a couple gradually lose the zest they once displayed? The freshness of their union wore off, and distance and strain became apparent. Such things as the gentle word, the tender touch, and the thoughtful looks perished. These things cannot happen if we love at all times, under all circumstances. Do you catch the tones of initiative and responsibility in the harmony lines of Solomon's statement, as I do?

Mark and Darlene's marriage illustrates this. Mark had a miserable childhood. He didn't learn to verbalize his love or his frustrations; furthermore, his parents had abused him. And then he married a sensitive woman who had learned the art of revealing most everything going on within her. Although Mark wanted more of what Darlene had in the way of freedom and self-disclosure, he was resistant to her graciously stated suggestions.

For twenty-one years he resisted her enduring support, thinking she was only trying to make him be like her. Finally, wanting to change, he sought me out. He spelled out his background and problem, and offered me a summary of the things Darlene had said to him over the years. As we talked further, I realized that Mark was threatened by her suggestions because "she's a woman and can't possibly understand what a man needs to do to become expressive." Her sustained love was rejected.

Believing Darlene's counsel had been on target all along, I sold Mark on the idea of becoming open to her thoughts and even going so far as experimenting with them. He consented, although with reservations. Recently he shared with me his surprise. "What she's suggested is working," Mark said, "I wish I had listened to her earlier." Her steady love paid off.

What happened? Mark needed someone outside the relationship to validate Darlene's thinking, to say it was good and sound counsel even if it was from his mate. My validation allowed him to listen to her. Sometimes I wish mates would listen to the good word of their mates—faithful mates whose suggestions only rise from love and true devotion. To some of you I am saying, "Listen to your husband or wife's counsel and don't write it off as something appropriate only to the opposite sex or to some other personality type. Perhaps the suggestions hold the key to some significant growth in your life!"

Adhesion . . . "Sticks closer than a brother." Solomon said it this way: "A man of many friends comes to ruin, but there is a friend who sticks closer than a brother" (Proverbs 18:24). The last five words of that statement are never so meaningful as when someone actually does stick closer than a brother . . . especially when for them it is hard, awkward, and unpleasant to do so.

The term *stick*, though as simple as the word *all*, gives us nearly as many problems. When tension sets in, it's easier to run than stick. The term means "to adhere to or bond."

Within the context of human relationships, the word describes one's *clinging to someone else with love and loyalty.* This is the way it is used in Genesis 2:24, "a man shall leave his father and his mother, and shall cleave [literally, *stick*] to his wife."

One of the ugliest scenes on the marital stage develops when a person turns against his spouse, detaching himself from the person God holds him responsible for loving. Sometimes it is subtle and seemingly harmless. Other times it is not. I have observed many husbands (and wives) who've resorted to making their spouses the objects of cruel jokes in the presence of others. They've belittled, embarrassed, even harassed them. While some are victims of physical abuse, just as many are recipients of verbal and emotional abuse.

Now, for some, their style of detachment is different, less aggressive. They become stone silent, ignoring their mate as though he or she were not present or did not exist.

Why does this occur? How can mates resort to such tasteless, ugly treatment? Numerous reasons exist, such as:

- Forgotten or ignored responsibility before God
- All-out abandonment of loyalty and kindness
- Insensitivity, or a refusal to understand the other person's problem, weakness, or pain
- Failure to see that a problem actually exists

Walking off, walking out, and walking away are not movements of friendship. They are directions of irresponsibility and neglect. Desertion of any sort (emotional or physical) scars friendship. It is my opinion that anyone who chooses to abandon another living soul made in the likeness of God has little or no capacity for authentic, meaningful, biblical friendship.

The Way to Build a Close and Permanent Friendship

Oneness, durability, and adhesion—the hallmarks of friendship—also serve as indicators to tell us whether or not a relationship is healthy. The question we now must ask is, *What do we do to cultivate a marital friendship that results in these qualities?* The Bible, practical as it is, provides us with at least seven replies to that question. Let's work our way through each one together.

Relate face to face. Face to face is where the process of building a friendship begins. Our faces are necessary focal points in our relationships. If we turn our face aside, we temporarily shut the door to continued growth. In the Scriptures, God has provided us an example that involves himself, one which we can imitate in our homes.

After Moses had led the Jews away from Egypt and into the wilderness toward their homeland, God met with him frequently just outside the camp in a place called the tent of meeting. When Moses made his way to the tent, the people stood at the entrances of their homes as he passed by. Once he entered the tent, the pillar of cloud (which guided the Israelites by day) dropped down in front of the entrance to guard it. While inside, "the LORD used to speak to Moses *face to face*, just as a man speaks to his friend" (Exodus 33:11, emphasis added).

The Hebrew word *face* used here always appears in plural form, indicating the *multiplicity of features constituting a face.* A person's face identifies him to others. It is the vehicle that projects his sentiments and attitudes, that displays his moods and emotions. We cannot intimately know another person apart from relating to his face.

When God met with Moses, he showed these things of himself to a human who was the product of his creation. In turn, he allowed the man to show him these same elements. Observe what Exodus 33:1-11 reports about this meeting:

- God *met* Moses, his friend, in his own surroundings.
- God, being the stronger of the two, *took the initiative* in relating in face-to-face fashion.
- God *accepted* whatever Moses was capable of giving in return (in spite of the inequity that existed between a sovereign God and a sinful man).
- Both God and man *revealed* themselves to each other.

This is precisely what husbands and wives must do together if they want to broaden their friendship.

Perhaps this is a good time to ask how long the two of you can look eye-to-eye comfortably without saying a word. Five . . . ten . . . fifteen seconds, or more? Approaching the twenty-second mark, discomfort usually sets in; by then we have become ill at ease—probably because we are feeling exposed. I've found that many people adjust to bodily nakedness more quickly than to emotional transparency. We avoid letting anyone see too much of us, particularly all at one time. At times it is because we aren't really prepared to see too much of the real person to whom we're married and with whom we share our bed.

Why is it that when individuals marry, eye contact falls by the wayside? If it helped to foster the friendship leading to marriage, then it should continue so that the marriage can ascend to the heights of maturity.

Candee and I love restaurants, as do many of you. Do you often marvel—as we do—how a plate of food can hold a person's attention spellbound for the duration of a meal? Next time you go to a restaurant, try an experiment. Count the number of people you see who sit across from each other without ever looking up into each other's eyes. The results will surprise you.

We have found that mealtimes in our family have provided us with some of the best moments for exchanging our hearts. It's no wonder that so much New Testament fellowship was centered around mealtimes, or "love feasts," as they were called.

I have stressed this point, but for good reason. If mates do not interact face to face, they won't take the other steps properly. This is the starting point of a close friendship.

Communicate with honesty. Frequently I am approached by couples who ask me to help them unravel the problems straining their ties. Usually the wife seeks help first. She hurts. Despair has become her daily diet. She sees no hope in sight. Many of you are at that point right now: You feel desperate. In counseling, the wife unloads each item from her emotional basket. She organizes her piles of pain, frustration, disillusionment, and anger . . . especially her anger. Customarily I ask, "Does John know about this? Have you told him what you've told me? What has been his response?" Invariably I hear something like, "No, not exactly. If I told him, he would be devastated and angry."

Solomon has wise counsel for us who have trouble communicating our real thoughts in such circumstances. Listen carefully: "Faithful are the wounds of a friend, but deceitful are the kisses of an enemy" (Proverbs 27:6). There are three comparisons in that statement. Don't miss them.

faithfulness versus deceit
wounds versus kisses
friend versus enemy

Which side of the comparison best characterizes you at this moment? For many, the clue to healing has been found in this proverb.

Early in our marriage Candee and I learned that there was no substitute for honesty, even though it might be painful. Our first tendency was to avoid speaking the truth in order to keep peace and avoid further conflict. I'd like to convey to you who are not so convinced that honesty is the prerequisite for freedom in friendship and marriage. It is also essential for the development of trust.

Let's consider the term *wounds.* A wound is defined as "an injury to the body where skin or tissue is broken or torn, often resulting in a scar." Of course, Solomon was not referring to physical or emotional injury. But he linked honest communication with something that is sharp and stinging. Such wounding precedes healing. That is essentially what surgery is: wounding that results in repair and restoration.

How about the contrast? In this context, kisses only give the appearance of kindness. They give the illusion that something is well. They are like bandaids which themselves are clean and sterile, but when placed over an infected cut only create the appearance of something therapeutic having been done. Kisses gloss over the problems, whereas wounds attack them directly.

Admittedly, it is not easy to switch from kissing to wounding. But if it's friendship you want with your spouse, then the choices are limited. Let me add a caution: Wounding is of no value if it's backed by heartlessness or if it attacks the person instead of the issue. Simply put, wounding is honest communication, confined to the issues, which never loses sight of the best interests of both mates.

Cultivate objectivity. Husbands or wives often turn to counselors for help when in fact their own mate might have been able help more effectively. It takes many sessions for a counselor (pastor or psychologist) to gather enough data to feel they can give suitable and objective advice. On the other hand, our mates have seen it all; they know us the best and usually have much to offer if given the chance. (I realize there are some exceptions, but I am talking in more-often-than-not terms.) For the most part it's pride that hinders the impact our mate could have on us. In my counseling experience, I find myself giving the same counsel or encouragement a mate has tried to offer all along. How do I know? Because the offending mate often has offered that information voluntarily.

Again Solomon is a help to us: "As in water face reflects face, so the heart of man reflects man" (Proverbs 27:19). Though the term *reflects* does not appear in the Hebrew text, the thought is definitely implied. Something reflected is "mirrored or given back in its exact likeness." Some interpret this text by saying that a man's or woman's heart is reflected by his own eyes, that what is deeply and essentially him is mirrored through his face. Though that is true, I believe the context of the proverb suggests something different. Instead of one person being present, there seem to be two. Water has no face of its own; it only throws back the image placed above it. In the proverb, water and heart are represented as having similar capabilities. The point is this: One person's thoughts and feelings are reflected back to him through interaction with another heart. This is objectivity in operation.

Let me personalize this for you. Often in our own relationship Candee or I need to know how we come across to others. We need to hear how our concerns sound to the one receiving our statements.

When we first began going to each other for mirroring or reflecting, we had some hurdles to overcome—particularly when we were the one being invited to do the reflecting. The problem was that the mirroring mate had already suffered to some extent from the problem the other mate needed to see; thus he took the opportunity to send back his own message of reproof or criticism. Instead of reflecting, he was getting even or letting his defenses hang out. That chilled the process immediately.

Because we wanted this mirroring to take place in our friendship, we finally adopted some protective guidelines:

- Don't confuse the invitation to mirror with an opportunity to get your strokes in. Those strokes are no longer necessary because your mate has openly come to you for reflecting.
- Report only what your eyes and ears have seen. And as you report it, stay within the limits of grace and kindness.
- When you violate either of these guidelines, quickly apologize and return to the guidelines.

It's that simple!

A word to the one who is seeking the reflection: If you ask for it, then accept it. Don't react, don't get defensive, don't argue. Just listen to the information and keep your responses in check. Take a few days to rethink what you've been told, and ask God to soften any hurt that has accompanied the truth. Ask him as well to help you filter the information so you can stay focused on the heart of the disclosures made to you.

Know what I've learned? It's never done me any good to argue with my mirrors—whether they're made of glass or of heart.

Promote growth in one another. Proverbs contains another piece of counsel for those concerned about building friendship: "Iron sharpens iron, so one man sharpens another" (Proverbs 27:17). Add in the word *mate* and read it this way: ". . . so one mate sharpens another." Think of it in those terms as we proceed. The tone of this proverb, by the way, is not one of fun. Yet a good friendship cannot blossom apart from its guidance.

In the process of sharpening, friction occurs and heat is produced. Arguments, or *discussions* (as I prefer to call them) are acceptable if they remain issue oriented rather than person oriented. *Sharpening* has the idea of "creating a fine edge, developing clarity." Some of the beneficial results of our two lives having rubbed together are healthier attitudes about God, family, friends, and self; more balanced dispositions toward life, job, and church; and a more tolerant outlook on pain, conflict, pressure, and inconvenience.

Only a precious few marriages find that growing together comes easy. Most of us, apart from sharpening, would remain dull, boring, unattractive, even useless.

And what should happen inside a union should happen also between various unions. Today the life Candee and I share has a finer edge because God has drawn us and a dozen other couples together weekly to discuss issues related to friendship and romance. In the five years we have been together, each has noticed radical growth in the other. Why? Because each has been "sharpened" by twenty-plus other perspectives. Husbands have learned from other husbands' wives. Some have learned that their own wives are not abnormal or emotionally unbalanced. Others have even come to realize their views of their wives have been unwarranted and based on ignorance. Wives, on the other hand, have learned that their husbands were not intentionally withholding expressions of their feelings, but like many of the others, they'd never been properly educated in the language of emotion. Besides this, we all discovered that our struggles were not unique. What a comforting thing to know!

Disclose your most private thoughts. It surprises me that people can live together twenty-five years or more without really knowing each other. But all too often it happens.

Frequently wives, for example, have no idea what their husbands earn or how they spend their day at work or where they go on their day off when they leave home by themselves. On the other hand, some husbands know very little about what their wives do during the day or about the people with whom they spend their time.

We have been attracted to a dimension of friendship that surfaced in Jesus' relationship with his treasured men, "his friends." As we review this part of his life in order to learn from him, let's keep in mind that he was God incarnate (literally, dressed in skin) relating to finite, imperfect men—men looked down upon by their contemporaries. Jesus looked past their surface to their true stuff.

Perhaps there were many other masters in his day instructing their own bands of students, but notice what he said of his men: "No longer do I call you slaves, for the slave does not know what his master is doing; but I have called you friends, *for all things that I have heard from my Father I have made known to you*" (John 15:15 emphasis added). He didn't have to do that; God's plan wouldn't have changed. He could have simply given them instructions without explanations. Instead, he chose to tell them the whole story. Why? Because those men were of great worth to him personally. Thus he opened his closeted thoughts to all of them.

Numerous times while dining with other couples, Candee and I have had the following phenomenon take place. In the midst of the conversation the husband reported a significant decision he had made affecting not only his life, but his wife's as well. The wife's jaw dropped in surprise, only for us to realize he'd never informed her that there was even a decision in the making. Because of embarrassment, the wife kept quiet so that she wouldn't look more ignorant. In each instance, the husband didn't care enough to include his wife in the making of the decision; he did not give her the privilege of offering to him her counsel and perspective. There can be no greater way of stating "You are an unnecessary adjunct to my life." Excuses like, "I forgot to tell you; I was busy; we haven't had much time to talk," are totally unacceptable. They are powerless to erase the pain caused by exclusion. When mates are important to us, we include them in all dimensions of our lives.

In all fairness, we must add this one thing: Some wives have ruined this openness by always criticizing their husband's thinking or by passing premature judgment on their proposals. They have driven their husbands into secrecy. If that has happened, they need to reestablish the atmosphere for such interchange.

Set aside your own comforts. In Jesus' second farewell address, he said to those who had been with him the past three years, "Greater love has no one than this, that one lay down his life for his friends" (John 15:13). This statement may poke hard at some of us. The term *lay down* conveys the thought of sincere self-sacrifice. It has the idea of putting aside personal desires and comforts for someone else's benefit. This instruction can't be left to lie in some ancient passage of Scripture. It must be integrated into our own naturally selfish lives.

I often find mates looking at marriage not as friendship, but as a competition—keeping score of how many times "I gave in and you didn't—you owe me one." Succumb to that and you know misery in its ugliest form.

A statement more articulate than the words "I love you" is the act of self-sacrifice. It says,"I care about you. You are invaluable to me. I do this out of love." Mates, take care to sharpen your ability to see sacrifice when it's made on your behalf. Don't allow it to pass without recognition. Say "thanks," and then give a reason why that sacrifice means something to you. You enhance friendship by expressing appreciation. Self-sacrifice must be acknowledged unless you want its motivation to fade.

Are you wondering what items in your life would be worth setting aside (or renegotiating) in order to enhance friendship with your spouse? Ask him! Your mate is the only one with the right answers. In the meantime, here are some of the things you might hear.

Men: The weekly priority of raquetball, tennis, golf, or sailing; the unwavering commitment to Monday night sports or the evening news; the inflexibility of your eighty-hour work week; the demand for silence when returning home from work.

Women: The need always to have everything perfect; the demand of having love and romance expressed only in terms acceptable to you; the inflexibility of the Saturday "to do" list.

Whatever it is your mate feels has become more important to you than the relationship is not worth the distance it has created. Be courageous and shove to the side the things that by nature keep you apart, the involvements that keep you in contact with others more than with your spouse. Remember, none of these things will wrap their arms about you in your old age. Only the love and friendship of your mate will provide you the soul comfort for which your heart longs. In the final analysis, so many of these things are hindrances to good love affairs.

Give your full support. There is one more thing we can do to cultivate friendship in our marriage. In dealing with this particular one, let's draw from the experience of Job. Periodically we say someone has the "patience of Job." Job was indeed patient, but our opinion of that patience will rise with our understanding of what he endured.

Job was married, with three sons and seven daughters. His portfolio included 7,000 sheep, 3,000 camels, 500 pair of oxen, 500 female donkeys, and "many" servants. Don't just read that without pausing a minute to imagine all those figures entailed. Much hardship and stress are associated with the rearing of ten children. Much time, energy, long hours, and sacrifice went into the development of his estate. All the time he was accumulating his assets, he was busy working to maintain and preserve them.

Now imagine this: *instant and total loss.* All of it vanished. He and his wife lived with the vacuum once filled by ten beloved offspring in whom they had invested themselves. Their memories must have kept their throats choked as they fought back the tears.

Up to this point the losses were shared. His wife had been touched to the extent he had. But then Job succumbed to a serious infection which covered his skin with boils. The disease was so putrid that he was forced to take up temporary residence in a refuse dump. He was terribly ill amid his grief . . . his wife was healthy amid hers. Their grief, though it could have been, was not shared. With this backdrop, let's recall his words: "For the despairing man there should be kindness from his friend; lest he forsake the fear of the Almighty" (Job 6:14).

When we read his wife's earlier statement, his term *despairing* takes on added weight in our minds. She said, "Do you still hold fast your integrity? Curse God and die!" (Job 2:9). When he was down, she shoved her heel into him, causing him further despair. It's interesting to observe how the terms *despair* and *garbage* are akin to each other in the Old Testament. In the dump he was coping with garbage within as well as without.

This illustration speaks for itself. When one is down, the other must come alongside him with acts of genuine friendship.

A Concluding Word

Under all circumstances we must move in toward each other, and in doing so as friends we must relate face to face, with honesty, cultivating objectivity, promoting growth, disclosing our hearts, making sacrifices, and giving support. Who knows, the final outcome may not only result in the greatest pleasure known to two human hearts, but at some point it might prevent a beloved mate from "forsaking the fear of the Almighty." Perhaps the lack of all these qualities adds up to one major reason some mates have not yet included Christ in their lives.

If you have friendship today, then work tenaciously to preserve it. If not, then begin taking the necessary steps so the two of you can enjoy again the very thing that brought you together in the first place.

Reflection

Whereas mature romance is the heart of marriage, friendship is the heart of romance. Without friendship, one of the fundamental ingredients of a healthy marriage is absent.

Generally speaking, couples who found their friendship to be pleasurable during courtship married in order to sustain that friendship. Yet with the passing of time, many have watched it succumb to pressures and responsibilities of shared living.

Since a friend is the one who stands on the same side of the struggle with you, then you and your mate need to make sure that you are both growing together in all aspects of your relationship . . . on that same side. Therefore when the struggles come, you're battling them shoulder to shoulder. This requires a lifetime of commitment.

Remember, true marital friendship is like sound health. You don't want to wait until it's lost before understanding its true value. Consider it valuable now as you nurture and protect it with all your might and soul! That alone is worth more in this life than all the things you can acquire.

Steps for Marital Growth

- ♥ Evaluate the friendship dimension of your marriage. What do you think has made it that way?
- ♥ Develop a definition of friendship with which you're comfortable. Remember, if a specific idea of friendship isn't clear in your own mind, it will be hard to maintain your relationship.
- ♥ There were three hallmarks of friendship developed in this chapter which were based upon a biblical phrase:

  Oneness . . . "Who is as your own soul"
  Durability . . . "Loves at all times"
  Adhesion . . . "Sticks closer than a brother [or sister]"

  Thinking your way through each one, measure yourself and ask, How am I doing? Careful evaluation leads to responsible changes!
- ♥ What kinds of things are you presently doing to cultivate friendship with your mate?

5

Understanding:

The Climate for Growth

Joan is a middle-aged woman whose ability to love her husband had been severely impaired. Time had callused her once sensitive heart. Perhaps her story is not uncommon, but the final outcome is so rare that I found myself captivated by her own unexpected discovery. I'll let Joan speak for herself:

> Four months ago, sitting in bed and feeling pity for myself, I took in hand a Bible my friend had given me to read. I was shot through with disgust because for some time my husband had failed to finish certain projects around the house. When he came to bed he received my half-hearted kiss. With his back to me, he fell asleep while I read. The words of Scripture that night touched me as in no other. Feeling both relieved and refreshed, I stood at the side of the bed slowly and deeply inhaling breaths of the freshest air I'd ever taken from the space in that room. I felt cleansed throughout. As I moved about the room, my attention was drawn to the eyes of my husband. They were

> marred by dark circles. At that moment, I was seized by the reality that those circles were there because he was tired from trying to survive the demands that I and the kids had put upon him. I began to feel so much love for him because I saw that it was his love for us that drove him to exhaustion to provide not only what we needed, but also all those other things we wanted as well.

Maybe you are wondering what passage of Scripture crowded her into that particular corner of reality, because you'd like to slip it to your mate in order to achieve the same result. Sorry! Joan can't remember the text that made its way to her heart that night. The only thing she knows is that God has wiped away a blindness that had kept her from seeing what a wonderful person had been lying alongside her nightly for years.

Let me ask you a penetrating question: When was the last time you caught a glimpse of your mate that stirred your love as Joan's love was stirred? Can you even recall such a discovery in your own relationship?

I wish that the insight born that night in Joan's bedroom could spill into every bedroom of every couple throughout the land, as well as into kitchens, living rooms, and dining rooms. That evening Joan experienced the birth of understanding. Sensitivity came to life . . . empathy rolled out of bed! The long-term disgust she had harbored toward her husband finally gave in to acknowledgment of the love her husband had demonstrated to her by clocking in and out at work day after day in order to provide for her needs.

For some of you nothing more needs to be said. Joan's experience can readily become your own. Others, however, may need more help to see how such sensitivity, hope, and love can enter their marriage. Let's consider how this is done.

The Way Homes Are Built and Relationships Are Established

A good illustration of straight counsel is documented in Proverbs 24:3-4. This statement should be inscribed over the entrance to every Christian home. If it were taken seriously and lived out, I believe the divorce rate among us would drastically diminish.

As we review this ancient yet timely advice, picture it as a set of threads to be woven throughout the fabric of your relationships. Here is the statement:

> By wisdom a house [relationship] is built, and by understanding it is established; and by knowledge the rooms are filled with all precious and pleasant riches.

If you pause and let those words talk to you, I think you will begin to see some things Candee and I observed several years ago . . . things which led us to engineer some necessary changes in the management of our own relationship.

We liked the tone of the words *built, established* and *furnished.* We wanted our relationship to depict them. About the same time that we happened upon these statements, we were involved together in the process of building an interior decorating business. God had opened up a door to a whole new world of color, texture, fabrics, accessories, and collectibles, and our thoughts were alive to the ideas of design, pattern, and arrangement. What a fun time it was in the life we've shared.

One day we saw that what you could do in a home to make it exquisitely comfortable and beautiful you could also do in a relationship. We wanted ours to be fully furnished and accessorized with nothing spared. Today we have redirected those interests toward helping others appoint their relationships with such furnishings as love and understanding. Because we wanted a built, established, and furnished kind of relationship, we began to pay attention to the activities associated with *wisdom, understanding,* and *knowledge.*

If you're not currently in the "home-building business" with your relationship, maybe establishing an acquaintance with these words will give you a blueprint from which to work. The first three words deal with phases of relationship, the second three with activities that make each phase possible.

First, the phase words. The term *built* identifies "the freshly completed result of putting together raw materials (wood, stone, mortar, and glass) and forming a structure or frame." This could easily describe the days of courtship leading up to and including the wedding ceremony.

Established has the idea of fixing something and giving it permanence. This corresponds to the first several years of marriage which are appropriately called the "adjustment years." Sad to say, many get caught in this phase—as in a carnival house with mirrored walls—and can't find the right exit out and into an open, comfortable, and intimate relationship.

The words *filled* or *furnished* describe the marriage when the right things have been accumulated and the relationship has been made a pleasant and secure place to dwell. This should constitute the rest of the couple's shared life, "till death do them part."

For those of you who are young in your marriages, my counseling experience these past years has underscored this one reality: *If failure occurs in the establishment phase, ultimately furnishing will never begin.* Joan is a living example of this. Many never seem to get beyond the problems of fighting for autonomy and control, of becoming victimized by fragile feelings, of being governed by unrealistic expectations, of being swallowed up by the other person's more dominant personality and nature, or of failing to resolve sexual difficulties. For all practical purposes, Joan's marriage had gone little further than the building stage, though she and her husband had been together nearly twenty years. But that one night resulted in the inauguration of a heartfelt marriage to her husband.

Let's look at the second set of terms, for they affect the progress of the first set. *Wisdom*, though used in a variety of ways in the Old Testament, has two ideas that are of interest to us. The first pertains to "skill" (it is used of the craftsmen who manufactured the tabernacle according to God's specifications . . . they were "wise" or "skilled"). The second deals with "perception," indicating the act of peeling away surface impressions in order to see life, circumstances, and people as God sees each. *Understanding* in its bare form means to know or grasp something completely. And *knowledge* describes the acquisition of facts and details, and for our sake pertains to every dimension of our mates' lives—their personality, heart, moods, dispositions, attitudes, dreams, and skills.

Wisdom and education don't always reside in the same people. That is, individuals who are highly trained are not necessarily skillful in the personal realms of life—marriage included. I think of Frank and Sharon as I say that because their situation has been duplicated by many others.

In their preadult years both did well in school, each was active in university life, and both were highly admired leaders among their peers. Sharon was academically brilliant, a bit more so than Frank, and she felt that she could lean on that brilliance to make everything work well for her. She felt that because she was skillful in handling information that she could apply that same skill to the structuring of a relationship and make her marriage successful.

Her interest was psychology. Whenever Frank would try to share his thoughts with her, she was quick to interrupt him and finish those thoughts for him. She would even tell him, "That's really not what you are feeling. Instead, you're feeling . . . ." Whenever he would defend the interests of his heart, she would discredit him for being "dishonest" about his feelings. She knew better, and she confidently played counselor to him through eight years of marriage.

Much to her surprise, information management and the managing of a growing friendship and romance were vastly different. As I watched their marriage disintegrate, I thought often how academic confidence can mistakenly be substituted for true and effective wisdom. Sharon began learning that when it was too late, when her second marriage was being drowned by the same substitution.

Let's think briefly about wisdom and its role in a marital romance. While the relationship is quite young, a husband and wife usually discover that a union of their two hearts does not develop immediately or automatically. Some never realize such oneness. Why? One reason is that wisdom is poorly exercised or even altogether absent. The relationship then functions amid confusion and mystery. Conflicts are many. Laughter is infrequent. Apart from exercising wisdom, we hinder the very growth we want to help along, and we injure the very love we want to inspire.

As with Frank and Sharon, most of us in our most needful moments are prone to hear what we *think* the other one is saying. We interrupt and try to finish the statements for him before he has the rightful pleasure of speaking his own mind in his own way and with his own words. Perhaps your own track record in this respect is lousy. You think you're on target with your guess when in fact you are so far afield that you have dealt a death blow to the conversation you both so desperately needed. This is just what Sharon did so well, failing to realize that every conversation should be treated with care. You see, each conversation we have together as mates really is another highway into each other's hearts.

Candee and I have come to believe and accept the fact that the only way to know what the other one is thinking or feeling is to allow him to speak for himself. This was very hard for me. I was the "Sharon" in our marriage for a long time. Only the one feeling something knows the depth and extent of his feelings. Today we see that if wisdom means "peeling away the surface to see what's underneath," then we must not get in the way of disclosure—by premature reactions—when one of us is reporting the movements of our soul to the other.

We found that most of our reactions anyway were connected only to the first few layers of disclosure, and that releasing them there only drove much-needed conversation off the road and into a hole. We've now learned how to repress those premature responses so we can get down into the important matters of our hearts and lives. If you haven't come to that discovery yet, do so now and begin applying it. It will make a great difference in the way your conversations move about.

The truth is that most of us do not lack the ability to be wise, but we are thin on the willingness to practice wisdom. It takes both effort and restraint to get below the surface and into the life of another person: restraint to avoid saying too much, terminating the conversation prematurely, defending ourselves when we're actually wrong; and effort to train our senses to remain alert at all times. Hearts are like so many other things: Their greatest treasures are safely protected well below the surface. Wisdom is the tool we use to dig them up where they can be viewed and enjoyed.

To those of you who are good with words, may I express this concern: In each couple there is usually one who is better at expressing his thoughts and ideas. The hazard of having such a God-given ability is that under pressure it can easily be misused. Good talkers are normally the winners of arguments and debates, whether they are right or wrong. However, good talkers don't necessarily demonstrate wisdom. If your mate struggles to communicate his or her concerns, then perhaps you have the greater responsibility to see that an atmosphere of wisdom is created and preserved. Ask God to give you grace to be silent and the desire to be affirming so that the treasures within the one you love can emerge and intensify the union of your hearts.

Once wisdom is exercised, then how is understanding made possible?

Practical Thoughts on the Establishment of Understanding

As understanding strong-armed its way into Joan's life that night, she entertained a wonderful set of feelings which were desperately needed. However, that was only the beginning. She had to build upon that event. She had begun to see life through her husband's eyes. Next she had to develop patterns of understanding that would become a way of life for her.

How do any of us pull that off? Sometimes by finding simple reminders. For that reason, I've selected three familiar words to help us in the development of understanding or empathy: *stop, look,* and *listen!* Perhaps in the days ahead, every time you cross a set of railroad tracks and see the crossing sign, you will think of the following reminders.

Stop! Understanding was not born within Joan until she stopped all her motion and activity. She quit churning and wrestling. She took off her disgust and hostility and laid them aside. She ceased what she was doing and became quiet.

Recently my young son Timothy followed me around the house trying to tell me something in his three-year-old style. As happens periodically, I was preoccupied in my thirty-eight-year-old style. Candee said to me, "Ed, why don't you stop and acknowledge him. Both of you will be happier." "That's true," I replied. For her the suggestion was simple: "Stop and acknowledge." But for me to do so was painfully difficult at that moment. I had just come home from work; I was weary and wanted a moment to myself. I didn't want to get entangled in anything that was going to put demands on me. Though I love my little guy dearly and thoroughly enjoy his friendship and love, that night I wasn't ready to be available. My wife's look was foreboding, so I gave Tim my attention. The result was actually wonderful . . . for both of us.

Stopping required two things: First, I had to cease my physical movements; second, I had to cease my mental movements as well. I realize that what you do with children, you do with anyone else. Your first step toward understanding is to stop all motion.

Look! Around our home, we've learned that until someone is looking at you and into your eyes, they are not going to understand you. Candee and I have learned that about one another. There have been times in our past when we sat down to talk and my eyes were on her, but she could tell they were glazed. I was looking, but I wasn't seeing. Looking is something we do actively. It's not just physical, but it is emotional as well. We are to look with both our eyes and hearts.

Rosalind Dymond, the psychologist who worked closely with Carl R. Rodgers in the fifties, called understanding and empathy "*the imaginative transposing of oneself into the thinking, feeling, and acting of another and so structuring the world as he does.*" That cannot happen apart from being wide-eyed. The term *empathy* comes from a German word, *Einfühlung*, meaning "to feel into." Another way of saying it: We empathize when we can see where someone else is and then put ourselves into his place (feeling what he feels and thinking what he thinks) as best we can.

One Sunday evening we arrived home at 9:30, only to find our home surrounded by half a dozen policemen. Besides the police there were several neighbors who were inside with our four children. Shortly before we had pulled up, a barefooted, barechested man had entered through a small pantry window and attacked our thirteen-year-old daughter, who was babysitting the younger ones. Though our home was well lit and obviously occupied, he made his way inside. Our younger daughter, who is fearless when threatened, came to her sister's aid and together the girls drove the intruder out before he seriously harmed either one of them. Now, the man took nothing tangible from our home as he fled into the darkness; however, he stole away from all of us our feelings of safety and security, feelings we have always prized.

For the girls the loss was more severe because they had had physical contact with the person. For many months they would not sleep anywhere else but at the foot of our bed. They wouldn't even go to the front or rear of the house unless accompanied by a parent, even in the daytime. As parents, it was easy for us to be tolerant of the situation. But after two months had passed, our patience began to experience fatigue. You see, never having gone through that experience firsthand, we had a hard time feeling what they felt. The same was true for their babysitters. The girls were the ones who had touched the criminal. We hadn't. To them he was flesh and bone, while to us he was an imagined character at best.

Often Candee and I have had to pause to ask Joy and Heather to reconstruct their individual feelings so we could get beyond our insensitivity. We've needed them to help us crawl into their bodies, as it were, to renew our feel for their unending seizures of fear.

Jesus Christ is described as one who understands us. He is our model. The lines of Scripture put it this way:

> "For since He Himself was tempted in that which He has suffered, He is able to come to the aid of those who are tempted" (Hebrews 2:18).

> "For we do not have a high priest who cannot sympathize with our weaknesses, but one who has been tempted in all things as we are, yet without sin" (Hebrews 4:15).

He looks and sees our inside struggle, and he can put himself and his feelings into us. In fact, the writer of Hebrews tells us as a follow-up to these statements, ". . . draw near with confidence to the throne of grace, that we may receive mercy and may find grace to help in the time of need" (Hebrews 4:16). What he does for us is precisely what we need to do for one another as husbands and wives, as friends with understanding.

Listen! Our last step toward understanding is to listen. All too often we feel obligated to talk back. Sometimes we simply need to listen. There are moments in our home when someone will say, "Don't talk. Just hold me and listen."

Listening may involve asking an occasional question, such as, "Honey, what is it that you wish I'd understand?" But apart from some clarifying questions, we need to be quiet . . . our ears need to be opened. No arguing. No defending ourselves. No discounting our mate's thinking and feelings. We need to just perform attentive ear-work. In fact, doing this all by itself could change most relationships.

Understanding mates are those who *stop, look,* and *listen!* How about you? If you and the one you love were given the opportunity to evaluate your level of understanding by these three criteria, would your assessments match? Or would you think you deserved a higher rating than your husband or wife would give to you? We ask you these questions:

- How close have you come to truly sharing your mate's feelings the way he's experienced them?
- Is there anything you need to do to shorten the gap between your heart and his to increase that sharing?

What a comforting touch is to the flesh, understanding is to the human heart. Listen to what Dr. Paul Brand and Philip Yancey say in their book *Fearfully and Wonderfully Made*:

> We have called touch a "basic" sense, but that word can mislead. Actually, touch is one of our most complex senses. . . . The elaborate mechanisms producing touch, for instance, prepare the skin to adapt to changing surfaces. Bioengineers use the word *compliancy* to denote this response. Compliancy describes the capacity of skin to flow around whatever surface it contacts, a quality skin exhibits better than any comparable material. Compliancy gives the body freedom to move and keep an unbroken, protective surface. . . . If my skin tissue had been made harder, I might insensitively crush a goblet of fine crystal as I hold it in my hand; if softer, it would not allow a firm grip. When my hand surrounds an object—a ripe tomato, a ski pole, a kitten, another hand—the fat and collagen redistribute themselves and assume a shape to comply with the shape of the object being grasped. This response spreads the area of contact, preventing localized spots of high pressure, limiting stress while giving firm support. . . . The compliant tissues covering my bones assume the shape—awkward or smooth—of the object. I do not demand that the object fit the shape of my hand; my hand adapts.[1]

That's a perfect description of what the compliant touch of understanding can do to a marriage relationship. It can prevent "localized spots of high pressure." It can "limit stress while giving firm support." It can adapt to "the shape" of the other human heart that is next to us. Truly understanding mates do not demand that their wife or husband change the shape of his suffering heart to fit their own, but instead they adapt their heart to fit the one who is in need of understanding and empathy.

Are you short on understanding these days? If so, then *stop, look,* and *listen!* Stop your motion and activity . . . quit churning and wrestling. Look into the soul of your mate with both your eyes and heart. Apart from an occasional clarifying question, listen to what your husband or wife is trying desperately to tell you . . . be quiet.

---

1. Paul Brand and Philip Yancey, *Fearfully and Wonderfully Made* (Grand Rapids: Zondervan, 1980), pp. 130-133.

Remember:

> By wisdom a house [relationship] is built, and by understanding it is established; and by knowledge the rooms are filled with all pleasant and precious riches.

Reflection

The oneness of marital friendship must begin somewhere in the vicinity of understanding.

Understanding comes alive when vision and hearing are working at their best: seeing life through each other's eyes and hearing the precise concerns of each other's souls during our most clumsy attempts to express them to each other.

This vision and hearing can only operate when we exercise both restraint and effort. Restraint to avoid talking too much when our mates are sharing their thoughts and feelings. Effort to train our senses to remain alert at all times so we can pick up the various signals they are sending to us.

Both restraint and effort make possible the activities that produce understanding, activities summarized by the words *stop, look, and listen.*

And those who learn to stop, look, and listen draw their mates' hearts into their own, creating the climate for further growth.

Steps for Marital Growth

- Reviewing Proverbs 24:3-4, personalize the text by putting yourself into it. Rewrite it as a guideline you can live by.
- Which stage of development best describes your marriage: *built, established,* or *furnished?* If the word you selected was one other than *furnished,* what has kept you from moving into that stage?
- A solution to insensitivity or misunderstanding was summarized in three familiar words: *Stop, look,* and *listen.* Which of the three gives you the most difficulty?

6

Distinctions:

The Qualities That Temper a Union

When we first noticed Wayne and Linda, we saw a couple that was quite attractive, in fact stunning. But we noticed a peculiar thing about them every time we saw them together: She always walked several feet ahead of him. As time passed and we observed more closely, it became apparent that he had a distressed look in his face as he followed her—whether they were leaving church, the market, or the restaurant. We frequently saw them all about town. When we got to know them a bit, we found out that she was always downplaying what he did and said. He could never quite be what she wanted him to be. Soon we realized she even determined the way he should dress and style his hair. Wayne was almost a non-existent entity in that marriage.

One day I learned that this man was the president of a very successful food chain in the metropolitan area. He was astute, pleasant, and managed a sizable work force. His stores were emerging everywhere. But even though he was a well-above average, well-liked person, his wife wouldn't see in him what others were seeing. When they met, she saw in him a man who could give her the luxuries she wanted, so she married him and set out to fix him up to be the nice-looking male prop she needed on her stage of life. Concerned about trying to keep his marriage together, Wayne did everything he could to adapt to her wishes. And whatever distinctions he possessed as a person were lost.

For one reason or another Linda classified Wayne's distinctions as worthless. Because his ways were not like hers, she viewed him as an oaf and set out to refashion everything about him to please her likes and dislikes.

Let's look beyond Wayne and Linda's relationship and think through this whole realm of distinctions and the effects that can occur in our relationships when distinctions are overlooked.

Our Worth Boxed Up by Labels

Something in most of us passionately resists being typed or categorized. Yet that hasn't stopped others from doing that to us. And ironically, it hasn't hindered us from doing the same to them. Someone has said that people have one thing in common: they are all different. Yes, that's simple but true!

Haven't you found that your friends, children, employers, employees, neighbors—including your husband or wife—have all tried their hand at classifying your personal characteristics and traits? Perhaps you are like me in that when you sensed their doing this, you resented it. Why? Because more often than not, predetermined values were attached to those assignments.

You see, typing usually creates for us a no-win, no-grow situation. We hate that. It gives us the feeling of being caged or pushed with our back to the wall. At times, too, you may have found yourself the victim of classifications that didn't really fit you. And when that happened, you quickly realized that your mobility was restricted and you could no longer complement or enhance the person you loved the way you would have liked. Why? Because their classification of you had discounted your worth in their eyes.

When our distinctions are brought together in marriage, we often view them as differences that threaten our personal identities. Then we tend to move to protect ourselves by issuing labels to our mates that have restrictive connotations. And like it or not, that's what they are: *restrictive*. Labels I've heard used frequently that do just this are *sanguine, phlegmatic, choleric, melancholic, free-spirited, ultraconservative, pragmatic*, and *emotional . . . emotionless*. Of course, there are many more, and you can fill in the blanks with those you've used or with those you've had used on you. But by now you have the idea.

Frequently a label may describe a portion of what we are. But the rest of what we are often gets lost in labeling; it could add pleasure and depth to our relationship if it weren't lost or buried by a misassigned title.

Sir Arthur Eddington, an astute English astronomer who lived around the turn of the century, said:

> We often think that when we have completed our study on one, we know all about two, because two is one and one. We forget that we still have to make a study of *and*.

Now, it's the knowledge and acceptance of *and* that is the recognition of our uniquenesses—those marks of distinction we each possess. It is also our allowing those distinctions to take their proper places in the relationship we share in common, leaving none out in the cold to die.

Linda never realized that about Wayne. She never came to terms with the concept of *and* in their marriage. Perhaps that's why their marriage was dissolved last year.

A Fresh Look At Distinctions

If we're not clear on what distinctions are, then we won't do a very good job of preserving them. Candee and I see distinctions as those divinely implanted and humanly influenced qualities and traits we carry with us through life which make us different from one another and worthy of special recognition; those marks of personality that are unmistakably ours, and different from anyone else's.

Each distinction becomes highlighted when it is placed alongside another of a different kind. And together each becomes more individually beautiful in the other's presence. One man has described the value of diversity in color, and what is true for color is true also for distinctions. He writes:

> A color on a canvas can be beautiful in itself. However, the artist excels not by slathering one color across the canvas, but by positioning it between contrasting colors or complimentary hues. The original color then derives richness from its milieu of unlike colors.[1]

Ah, this is precisely what God desired to do as he brushed our distinctions onto the commonly shared canvases we call our marriages. Look at it this way. Your special combination of these unique traits results in texture, dimension, and form that constitute yet another amazingly priceless portrait of God's love. I want you to see that about your own relationship. Regardless of the kind of beginning you have had—stormy or otherwise—you and your mate constitute another creative, original portrait from God's brush. That is true in spite of what you've come to think and feel about yourselves and your union.

The problem is that many of us have little or no appreciation for such art. Thus we fail to see what is really there . . . to be studied and enjoyed by God's eyes, as well as our own. So what do we do? We treat each other with a diminished sense of worth. We shove each other aside like an old art object, tossed into the corner of a dusty attic to be forgotten. That's exactly the statement Linda was making by always walking ahead of Wayne. She'd shoved him aside long ago. In fact, her wandering eye reinforced that very thing.

Benefits or Differences?

As we said earlier, when we pair up in marriage, our distinctions become immediately noticeable. They can even be viewed as the kind of differences that threaten us and produce

1. Paul Brand and Philip Yancey, *Fearfully and Wonderfully Made* (Grand Rapids: Zondervan, 1980), p. 31.

an uneasiness which ignites competition and a battle for control of the relationship.

Candee and I found this was true for us in the early years of our marriage. Actually, the resulting tension kept us off balance with each other until we began seeing that our distinctions were jointly held assets rather than conflicting differences or liabilities.

From the beginning it was apparent that Candee was a visionary (notice I didn't say "dreamer") while I was a realist-pragmatist. Those are the labels I was using in those days. No matter what stood before us requiring some kind of a decision, these viewpoints emerged and went to war. They came out involuntarily. They needed no coaxing. Earlier in our union, we had no idea both characteristic outlooks were indispensable for making sound, enduring decisions. Each of us merely felt our own life approach was fundamentally right, the other wrong.

The result was that often we walked away from one another feeling despair and rejection, while the issue between us—actually that faced us together—was left unresolved. We wanted the other one to adopt our viewpoint . . . the right viewpoint!

One issue that remained a fertile battlefield for us was home decorating. We couldn't agree. Distinctively, Candee was anxious to spread paint and put up wall coverings to make the house a warmer place, a place that expressed our life together. I was busy figuring up the costs involved to see if it was practical. Now, though the expense was minimal, the issue in my mind was, "Should we spend our hard-earned money on some other man's rental, especially if we're not going to be here that long?"

All too often I won out, but not to our advantage. It's just that I was good at talking, and Candee got tired of fighting and defending the viability of her plans.

Finally, we purchased our own home, and Candee immediately began seeing how a few inexpensive improvements could be made to enhance our investment. You guessed it! Late at night, while she was asleep, I was off in a remote corner of the house penciling things out again to verify my viewpoint, "Why put much money in this place if we're not going to be here that long?"

It's interesting to me, now that I look back, to see that the real issue wasn't the money . . . it never had been. The underlying tension was the byproduct of three things for us: a failure on both sides to accept and respect each other's approach to life in general; a lack of knowledge that our distinctions could be harmonized into a shared perspective; and finally, a lack of trust for the other's potentially hidden motives behind the lobbying for our viewpoints and wishes.

I am pleased to tell you that today the realist-pragmatist has been tempered by the visionary, and the same is true the other way around. Candee and I now enjoy putting both perspectives to work on any given choice we decide to pursue. And added to that, we've put away the labels.

Your Marriage Is a Collage of Traits

My purpose in writing this chapter is to encourage you to see the value of accepting each other's distinctions; and instead of discounting or sequestering them, discover what they are so you can responsibly create the environment that will help them rise and flourish.

God has implanted certain sexual and individual qualities within us, while he has allowed others to develop from our home and cultural settings. In view of this, it is essential that we cease restraining each other. We must involve ourselves in decisively nurturing one another's continuing development within the bordering distinctions we both possess. If we do this, we'll find that it will have a liberating impact on our marriages, and on our relationships inside and outside our home. This particular focus will help many of you reestablish—or perhaps even establish for the first time—the harmony for which your hearts hunger.

When we marry, we toss an assortment of traits into the mixing bowls of our relationships. What are some of them? Well, one loves the sunset while the other prefers the sunrise. One takes neat, meticulous notes as the other scribbles his thoughts on the margin of his page . . . and slantwise, no less! While one is antsy, the other is relaxed. Invariably, one is a collector and the other a tosser. It's easier for one to give away money; it makes more sense to the other to give away time. One prefers to make love with soft, engaging music in the background, while the other is ill at ease with any sound at all—even a loving, spoken word.

Our struggle goes all the way back to the days of creation. The first man and woman were different from each other, bearing God-given distinctions that made them individually unique. The woman was not a carbon copy of man. And in the initial days, Adam and Eve were not in conflict, nor were they competing for control. God had created Eve and given her the desire to be a complement to her man. Adam was totally thrilled with the companion God had given him. God had assigned each one a repertoire of clear-cut distinctions (apart from their personalities) to make their marriage work.

Paul, in reviewing these, zoomed his readers' attention in on the interdependence of those distinctions. His statement is by no means comprehensive, but it deals with some fundamentals. He expressed it this way:

> In the Lord, neither is woman independent of man, nor is man independent of woman. For as the woman originates from the man, so also the man has his birth through the woman; and all things originate from God (1 Corinthians 11:11-12).

So what happened? Why has marriage become such a tense relationship?

When sin invaded human life, Adam and Eve's focus shifted, and this interdependence which had been taking into full account the survival and free-functioning of their distinctions was now threatened, not enhanced. Their distinctions didn't change. The purpose for the intermingling of those distinctions didn't change, either. But when sin entered, appreciation for the distinctions did change, triggering a battle for control.

At various points in history, the present included, interdependence and recognition of distinctions have been tossed aside by large portions of the populace—men and women alike. Today, the woman has been encouraged by her peer group and activist coalitions to take charge of her own life, marriage, and destiny . . . and to resist interdependence with her mate.

At the same time, the man has been told by his peers to preserve his dominance at all costs and protect his full roster of freedoms, even if it means that others around him pick up the price tag for his doing so. Incidentally, some men are finally waking up to the painful results of being suppressed and backed into a corner. Their wives have begun fighting back by playing the games of control without love (which should not be confused with leadership), dominance with little regard for the other's distinctions, and freedom without accountability.

When the first couple shoved aside God's guidelines for life and pursued what was for good reason off limits to them, their attention was diverted from God to self, and their concentration was turned from *you* to *me*. God's desired experience for them was sabotaged. Whether or not competition and manipulation besieged Adam and Eve's own union, we do not know. But quite possibly it did, considering the factors surrounding the way they fell.

The point is that one sex cannot exist apart from the other. One is not worth more and the other less. A man needs *everything* his woman brings to his life, and whatever percentage of herself either he or she suppresses causes a shortage in that relationship. The reverse is true also.

You Are a Unique Menu of Divinely Instilled Distinctions

Psalm 139 is a set of lyrics written by David and first sung around the tenth century B.C. This hymn drew the worshiper's attention to the comforting (and perhaps sometimes unsettling) fact that God was thoroughly and continuously knowledgeable of him and his way (v. 3). As you review this psalm, you'll see its message is intimate, its tone reflective, its ending introspective. The psalm opens with these words:

O LORD, Thou hast searched me and known me.
Thou dost know when I sit down and when I rise up;
Thou dost understand my thought from afar.
Thou dost scrutinize my path and my lying down,
And art intimately acquainted with all my ways.
Even before there is a word on my tongue,
Behold, O LORD, Thou dost know it all.
Thou hast enclosed me behind and before,
And laid Thy hand upon me.
Such knowledge is too wonderful for me;
It is too high, I cannot attain to it (Psalm 139:1-6).

Perhaps an understanding of a handful of words will unlock for you the meaning of this great text, just as it has for Candee and me.

First, as David spoke of his own ways that were the object of God's scrutiny and in-depth probe, he chose the term meaning "road or journey, lifestyle or manner." It was used to describe the personal patterns of his life that resulted from choices and attitudes and personality traits.

Lines later, David referred to the origin of those ways by saying:

For Thou didst form my inward parts;
Thou didst weave me in my mother's womb.
I will give thanks to Thee, for I am fearfully and
wonderfully made;
Wonderful are Thy works,
And my soul knows it very well (Psalm 139:13-14).

The Hebrew term translated *inward parts* literally means "kidneys." However, when used figuratively—as it is here—it speaks of the staging platform for our emotions, affections, and actions. It also refers to the innermost aspects of our personality. Here's where those divinely instilled traits of ours enter the picture.

Understand, not only was David alert to their presence, but he was mindful of the way they'd been introduced into his life. He wrote of how God had woven him in the womb, where a life is staged for nine months prior to being launched into the outside world. With all the ingredients on hand, God went to work interlacing material and nonmaterial ingredients as one does thread, yarn, twigs, flowers, and reeds. He teased them into, through, and among each other in order to make something both beautiful and useful. Through the eyes of his mind, David could see how God had fashioned him into an integrated being, bearing distinctions no one else possessed in his combination. He was a unique menu of traits.

Hmm! What the king-composer acknowledged about himself, we must also acknowledge about ourselves . . . and others, particularly our mates and offspring. They too are "fearfully and wonderfully" fashioned right down to the most subtle distinction stroked onto their cellular, "soul-ular" canvases. They're art, just as you are. And they are to be placed on display where they too have the same opportunity to be studied and enjoyed, just as you want to be. You see, we need to learn not only how to survive in the presence of each other's distinctions and differences, but we also need to become committed to preserving them.

Taking Them As They Come

It's not news to most of us that people enter marriage thinking they will change, or that they will be able to change their partner. But the surprise for many is that it usually does not work that way. At least, we don't immediately see the developments expected or hoped for.

I have appreciated the comments written by Judson and Mary Landis in the work, *Building a Successful Marriage*. See if you don't agree with them.

> The wedding does not change basic personality structure. If change occurs soon after the wedding, it is more likely to be that of people reverting to their real selves, when traits or tendencies that may have been suppressed or controlled during courtship become evident again. To marry with the idea that one will make changes in their spouse or his ways after marriage is to invite trouble. It is true that a good mar-

> riage promotes growth in both partners, so that over a period of time, people do change in many ways, but probably not in the kinds of ways that a hopeful fiancée may have in mind when she says, "That habit irritates me, but after we're married I'll get him to change." *The growth changes that occur under the impact of a good marriage will be gradual and will require time, sometimes a lifetime.* The changes will also tend to go in directions and remain within the limits set long before marriage by the . . . experiences of each person. For this reason, people choosing mates need to be alert to traits of marriageability or unmarriageability already developed in themselves and others [emphasis added].[2]

The truth is that many of us didn't really know our own distinctions until we moved out of our homes and territories and in with our husband or wife. Did you? There's something about marriage that strips away the illusions we pick up along the way. For the first time, we can make unvarnished comparisons. Amid the swirl of adjustment we find ourselves asking, What am I really like? How am I like others? How do I differ? Am I all right, or unacceptable? Should I like me the way I am? Or should I modify me in order to fit my mate or those about me?

Looking back, one snag Candee and I soon encountered in our own marriage was that our differences unsettled us. We first misconstrued unity and harmony for sameness. Honestly, don't we all do this with others also, like our children, our grandchildren, our parents, our friends, and the people we work with? The two of us do, much as we hate to admit it to you; and we are working continually to grow above this tendency with the everyday aid and conviction God's Spirit brings to our lives.

Ask yourself this question: How much of my time and energy is spent fretting over the fact that others do not see it my way or choose the things I prefer for them? Now, don't dodge the question. Its answer may tell you why you pick up the

---

2. Judson T. and Mary G. Landis, *Building a Successful Marriage*, 5th ed. (Englewood Cliffs, N.J.: Prentice Hall, 1968), p. 95.

impression from some that they are pulling away from you, why they are infrequently available when you call and ask them to do something with you.

A funny little thing happened around our place one day that illustrates this tendency to be unsettled by others' differences. This occasion involved one of our daughters. In the usual last minute grand prix to get everyone to school on time, Mom noticed Joy frantically leaving the house, sprinting to the waiting van as she dropped her lunch and several books along the way. Mom's focus was drawn to the lunch sack that had been grabbed from the counter, but whose top had not been folded over "the normal number of times." Little did we have time for the discussion that occurred over the rights and wrongs of open-topped lunch sacks.

Catching ourselves in the midst of an intense interchange, we suddenly realized that as adults we were forcing our preferences onto our daughter. And they were just that—preferences. There was no morality or spirituality at stake. Joy simply didn't mind carrying an unfolded lunch sack to school. That was her way . . . that was okay! Distinctively, she too has a practical streak in her, and she doesn't care how the food gets there, just as long as it makes it all the way to her desk. No big deal.

In reality, Joy adds a special, light touch to our family life and often helps us to chuckle when things get too serious. She does those things that help break the tension we live under so frequently.

You know, when we will allow another set of distinctions to bombard ours without fighting it (be it those of our children or those of our mate), and we let others be themselves in the process, something both beautiful and constructive will happen in our relationship with them. That bombardment of their traits upon ours eventually can effectively penetrate our tightly sealed world view and help us look out to see life and love in a fresher, fuller, and more varied way. It can even cause us to laugh instead of being so blasted serious all the time. And Lord knows, we need more of that.

We have been looking at the traits God has implanted

within us and have indicated that they come to us in two varieties: those linked to our sexual orientation—both physical and emotional—and those that are individual—simply those marks of uniqueness given to us apart from our male or female boundaries. But what about those distinctions, on the other hand, that come from man?

You Are Also a Unique Menu of Humanly Influenced Traits

Again, there are at least two varieties of distinctions that we inherit on the horizontal plane of life: ones that come from home and others which are cultural, picked up from those we relate to most frequently. Let's briefly consider each.

Home distinctions. When you carried away the last bags from the household where you were reared and dropped them onto the floor of your new place, you left behind sights, sounds, and smells of home that would never be experienced the same way again. However, you didn't leave behind everything. You did carry with you the traits your parents stamped on you. You pirated many of their patterns and mannerisms (and in our own case, we also pirated a sweeper, some tools, and . . .). Perhaps you have even found that you clean the way your mom did or didn't. You may have first favored the laundry products she preferred. You may even have mimicked the menus she prepared for you over the years.

In the beginning you probably managed your financial affairs the way your parents did—to the extent that you even tried to accumulate, in a brief period of time, what it took them a lifetime to gather. And if they were bargain hunters, you perhaps adopted their way until . . . until you caught a feverish appetite for opulence and excess which lasted until you had to admit that your income wasn't sturdy enough to support those appetites.

All this works for us, and those distinctions serve us well at the beginning of our marriages. But eventually we have to sort through those things to see what the two of us wish to keep or to shed in order to make way for those things we want to have characterize our new home. We have to find those that best suit us and take into account the unique blend of our personalities.

Now let's turn our eye toward our cultural distinctions.

Cultural distinctions. Few know just how different they are from other people until they get beyond their familiar geographical borders. Some have never been out of the state in which they were born. Others have been but a state or two away from home base. Yet they married someone who came from the other side of the country, who brought along with him unusual ways of thinking and doing which they found peculiar and perhaps threatening. Cultural differences have strained many relationships because mates could not figure out how to make them work to their advantage.

Dr. Paul Brand, a seasoned physician whose work with lepers has taken him to a variety of places in this world, describes a handful of distinctions he's encountered in just one slice of the world. As you read his words, you'll perhaps understand what we mean by cultural distinctions, and maybe you can see in a broader sense some differences about yourself that you didn't know existed. He writes:

> People, created in [God's] image, have continued the process of individualization, grouping themselves according to distinct cultures. Consider the continent of Asia for a crazy salad. In China women wear long pants and men wear gowns. In tropical Asia people drink hot tea and munch on blistering peppers to keep cool. Japanese fry ice cream. Indonesian men dance in public with other men to show that they are not homosexual. Westerners smile at the common Asian custom of marriages arranged by parents; Asians gasp at our entrusting such a decision to vague romantic love. . . . Many Asians begin a meal with a sweet and finish it with a soup. And when the British introduced the violin to India a century ago, men started playing it while sitting on the floor, holding it between the shoulder and the sole of the foot. Why not?[3]

3. Brand and Yancey, p. 32.

What the renowned anthropologist Ruth Benedict said of society in her book, *Patterns of Culture*, is true also of a marriage: "Society in its full sense . . . is never an entity separable from the individuals who compose it."[4] Such is the case for your union as well. The full sense of your marriage is composed of the uniquenesses each of you spills onto the new canvas of your relationship—cultural uniqueness included.

Your Shared Distinctions Make Your Marriage Like No Other

If you've tried to compare the state of your relationship and the quality of your union to that of acquaintances, more than likely you've become frustrated. It seems as though there is always at least one couple who appears to have it more together than you do. Now, although they don't, it appears they do. Something that helped me was the realization that no two marriages were alike, nor did they need to be. The only thing that mattered was that my marriage was making progress toward the potential maturity it was capable of achieving.

When our most recent couples group initially began, many of the couples had reservations about the experience. Why? Because each was quietly intimidated by the others. Here are some of the comments most everyone expressed at year's end:

> "At first, we looked around and thought that many of the people had near perfect marriages, and that we were out of place being here."
>
> "We felt that we lacked the maturity the others appeared to have."
>
> "We first thought we had nothing to offer the other couples."

It was exciting to see—actually within a few weeks—that we all had the same inner struggles the others had. In fact, some who thought they were nothing but weak discovered they had

4. Ruth Fulton Benedict, *Patterns of Culture* (New York: Houghton Mifflin Co., 1934), p. 253.

some strengths the others didn't possess. Each was behind in some areas . . . and ahead in others. Believe it or not, that's true for you also. Thus comparisons can only create unnecessary havoc in our lives.

It will help you to accept the fact that we're all different and distinct in a wide assortment of ways. And each time two of us join, we bring together all our distinctions—sexual, individual, home, and cultural, and while trading vows we form a unique union that cannot be separated from the individuals who reside in it.

That's what makes life interesting and colorful—though many view it as threatening. This is just as God wanted it to be from the beginning. Each marriage, in fact, has a resulting personality of its own because of this blending of distinctions.

Many who have studied marriage have tried to type the unions we all have made, but it really can't be done. Gary Collins, a man who has closely observed myriad marriages during his counseling career, gives us these reassuring words:

> Are there marriage personalities? It has been suggested that marriages, like individuals, have unique personalities. They are not all the same and neither can they be treated alike. At the time of marriage, the husband and wife each bring a unique set of values, beliefs, expectations, past experiences, personality characteristics, and "ways of doing things." These must be merged into some kind of working relationship which also considers social issues such as in-law influences, vocational demands, level of income and economic conditions or minority biases in the society. Although some writers have given creative descriptions of marriage types, it probably is as difficult to categorize marriages as it is to categorize individuals. No person, and no marriage, really fits the "type" category. Each is unique and this uniqueness must be remembered in counseling.[5]

5. Gary Collins, *Christian Counseling: A Comprehensive Guide* (Waco, Tex.: Word Books, 1980), pp. 176-177.

What I want you to see and acknowledge is that regardless of where you and your mate's uniquenesses come from, together you must work to create the kind of environment where your mate will thrive and bring benefit to your shared life. Of course, there may be certain distinctions that from time to time will need to be altered—not every distinction is good in and of itself. But for the most part I find that it is not so much the disposition of the negative traits that gives us the most trouble, but the acceptance of the broad range of our traits which is often overlooked in marriage relationships.

And once you begin to honor each other's full repertoire of distinctions, you will begin to experience something new—a tempering of your relationship.

Reflection

There is no need for us to be like each other, yet our tendency is to preserve our own distinctions while we bury the distinctions of those around us.

It is those divinely implanted and humanly influenced qualities and traits we carry with us through life that make us different from each other and worthy of special recognition.

One mate's distinctions are not worth more while the other one's are worth less. Fact is, both husband and wife need everything the other person brings into the relationship, and whatever percentage of those unique qualities are shelved or suppressed adds up to a loss the marriage can't afford.

Marriage was never intended to be a relationship of one personality, but one flesh . . . one soul. Therefore a major concern of caring mates should be to see that both persons' uniquenesses are given sanctuary so they can continue growing while adding life to their relationship.

Steps for Marital Growth

- What labels have you given to your mate in the past that may have restricted his worth in your own eyes? How has this influenced your relationship?
- What qualities has your mate wanted you to acknowledge within your marriage which you've been slow to honor?
- Which distinctions do the two of you possess that have caused you the greatest conflict? Take the one that's most prominent in your thinking, and find creative ways to change the tone surrounding it without altering the distinction itself.

7

Control:

The Force That Annihilates One's Love

Because we grow up without a proper understanding of differences and their importance to married life, we accept the faulty and restrictive guideline that says, "Only one way is right." We subtly believe that individuality is a weakness and conformity a strength. We think in terms of there being space for only one style, one opinion, one approach, one solution, and one expression to exist . . . "Mine, not yours."

When only one mate can be right, and yet two individuals occupy your marriage, something (or someone) has got to give. The question is who? One in your duo has no other option than to give in if harmony is to be maintained. They have to slip in and under the other person and blend into his shadow. The tragedy is that their uniqueness is either obscured, surrendered, or both.

So who gives in? It's certainly not the person who believes that control is a virtue or a special prerogative. Instead, it is the nonfighter or the peacemaker—the one who wants quiet and calm at any cost even though true peace may not be achieved . . . and usually isn't. It is often the mates who are least dominant, willing to give in because they don't do well in the battle—they are either unskilled warriors or orators. Some do not stand up for themselves in a wholesome sense, perhaps because they no longer treasure their own uniquenesses. They have been shoved down so long they have forgotten that they have any worth of their own. Frequently the mate who gives in is the one who is "nice," tolerant, and flexible.

My concern right now is for the person who must control every decision, approve every expenditure, choose every vacation option—who must have the upper hand in all movements of the relationship. An example of such a controller is what one man has called the "image-manager." John Gardner, a major business leader, activist, and consultant concerned about the worth and indentity of the individual, has said, "The image-managers encourage the individual to fashion himself (herself) into a smooth coin, negotiable in any market."[1] That doesn't just happen in the business arena, for dominant, misguided mates—husband or wife—can get involved in image-management easily if they shove aside the value of distinctions. God doesn't overlook their value, so neither should we . . . unless we want to place maximum stress on the marriages we have entered and kill the love affair that's just beginning to blossom.

Several years ago, Candee and I counseled an attractive coed who was finding her way back to the Lord she'd once loved. As she pulled her life together, a young Christian executive working for a large firm noticed her and began his pursuit. In a few months they were engaged.

Late one evening, a week prior to the wedding, she called us in tears and said she was so confused. Curt had suddenly begun putting immense pressure on her to change. He wanted Betsy to lose weight, dress differently, and restyle her laugh, which was offensive to him. This came as a surprise to us because she was

1. John W. Gardner, quoted in Laurance J. Peter, *Peter's Quotations* (New York: William Morrow and Company, Inc., 1977), p. 265.

already both winsome and beautiful. But something was seriously wrong. Her soon-to-be husband was infinitely more concerned about remodeling her visible features in order to enhance his own image among his tradesmen than with preserving the divinely ordained person to whom he was first attracted.

Against our counsel, she went through with the wedding and spent the early years of her marriage constantly and unnaturally trying to repattern herself to suit the man who wanted her to be his smooth, personless coin, "negotiable" in his particular marketplace. He was happy! She was not. Those years were needlessly tough because of his pride, self-centeredness, and above all his strong hand.

Many of us have engaged in image-management at one time or another. Unconsciously, at times we're given to playing God. We may reject this notion, but when push comes to shove, we have to admit that it is true. As we slip into it, however, we must realize that in doing so we selfishly seize control of someone and do to them what man has done to his aging world: We waste and deplete his resources . . . we strip-mine his life, leaving an empty crater behind. But at the time, you see, we aren't thinking that what we're doing today is determining the capacity of our future relationship, whether a decade from now it will be free or chained.

Making a Home Where Both of Us Reside

None of us can afford to forget that the purpose of marriage is not to become one personality, but instead to become one flesh, one soul. In marriage we are added up, not swallowed up. The suppression of distinctions and personalities through the misapplication of one's role or misuse of authority is *wrong*. It kills the feelings our relationships need in order to continue. It also destroys the sense of hominess we must find within our union that comes when *all* of the both of us is included and preserved in the marriage.

Barbara Lazear Ascher, in a piece she wrote for *House and Garden*, perhaps says it best:

> Home is the soul we wrap around ourselves, an outward display of our inner selves. Aspirations, affections, quirks and passions, bits and pieces of the past—as it was or we wished it to be—gone on parade within these walls.[2]

In many instances today, home is disappointedly wrapped about only one of us, while the other feels like an overnight guest in the relationship. In fact, go into many homes and you see this one-sidedness actually portrayed in the way the house is decorated or the remodeling job was done. Instead of looking like a joint expression of lives, it favors solely the man or woman of the home—*their home*.

In the same article, Ms. Ascher quotes Gloria Vanderbilt as saying: "All decorating comes out of our deepest feeling about ourselves, our beauty, and our hopes for ourselves."[3] Too many homes reflect only the presence of one expressed soul in a dwelling where two reside. Is that true for yours? It ought not to be, unless you have agreed to a solo expression.

An Identity Lost

Let's talk about swallowing up identities. When you consume or erase your mate's distinctions through dominance, manipulation, or force, or strip away her freedom to be herself under the auspices of "submission," you display your self-centeredness in its most notorious form. I can't find anywhere in Scripture that one is to *demand* submission of his wife, for example, to require of her that she wrap her whole life around every whim and wish that comes from his mind.

I am burdened because I've counseled many men who have taken the chain of command idea and used it as a weapon to keep everyone in their family in line—treating everyone as though they were indentured to his headship. In looking back at Ephesians 5:22-33, I definitely see a set of relationships laid

---

2. Barbara Lazear Ascher, "A Personal Tradition," *House & Garden*, February 1984, p. 76.

3. Ibid., p. 76.

down that have to do with the way Christ the Son relates to the Church, the way man relates to Christ, the way a wife relates to her man—and her man to her in return. But nowhere in those lines do I see severity or self-centeredness. Never is the one mentioned second in the sequence only to bring satisfaction to the first. What I do see is a marvelous mutuality that's often ignored by men who have an inordinate need to dominate and control.

Because of a hint from this text, my thoughts are drawn to the relationship God the Father had with God the Son. Nowhere is it more clear than in John 17, when Jesus was overheard by his disciples praying to the Father just hours before his trial and crucifixion. Thinking of the whole relationship as it is portrayed in the New Testament, the Father never lorded his position in the Godhead over his son. If anything, he went to great pains to elevate him in the eyes of the people he'd come to save. At Jesus' baptism—so that all present could hear—God said, "This is my beloved Son in whom I am well pleased." And sometime after that, as Jesus was speaking with his disciples, he identified the difference between him and his Father, but at the same time he underscored the mutuality of their relationship. He put it in these terms:

> Do you not believe that I am in the Father, and the Father is in Me? The words that I say to you I do not speak on My own initiative, but the Father abiding in Me does His works. Believe Me that I am in the Father, and the Father in Me (John 14:10-11).

In another instance he spoke of himself and his father as being "one" (John 10:30).

The point I want to reinforce is this: Just as the Father and the Son have two unique roles, and one is leader to the other, they embrace each other as one . . . the same way husbands are to do to their wives, and wives their husbands. There is a shared view and respect for the other's position. In marriage, the leader and submitter roles are primarily to be adopted in the midst of crisis when we come to impasses, but they are not dimensions that have to be operative every moment we're together. Fact is, the most dominant leader types can't shed those roles even when they're not called for. They think they have got to be in charge all the time or else they're abrogating their responsibilities.

Forced modification of a mate's personality and dominant, strong-handed control are enslavements and nothing else. But we often get by with them because they leave no physical bruises which an emergency room specialist can see and report. They do leave scars, however, on a mate's mind and emotions. Somehow Christian men have run wild with biblical teachings on submission and have run human life into the ground while trying to apply these teachings to their advantage. Christ himself must be appalled at much of what he sees his churchmen doing today to their women and kids. Men who take on the name of Christ and call themselves his followers are to live out one mandate that if taken seriously would shape all the other responsibilities they're called upon to fulfill in God's Word. That mandate? Paul casts it in these terms:

> Husbands ought also to love their own wives as their own bodies. He who loves his own wife loves himself; for no one ever hated his own flesh, but nourishes and cherishes it, just as Christ also does the church (Ephesians 5:28- 29).

Just as Christ loved the Church! That's hard for me to comprehend. When one of us takes seriously this guideline, he doesn't demand submission. He doesn't employ senseless control and manipulation to get the responses he wants out of his wife. Neither does she do that to him. Instead, he shows appreciation for all the submission and respect his wife grants to him—of her own doing—even when it's tough for her to follow his often immature leading.

I'm of the opinion that control is just another form of abuse that is still protected by acceptability in today's culture—in the church and outside it. Nonetheless, it has no place in a marriage relationship where it is claimed that God exists.

If anything is clear in Scripture about the tone of a marriage, it is this: Mates who care deeply about God and about each other pay attention to the priorities of *nourishing* and *cherish-*

ing, and at the same time they surrender to God their own control instincts . . . they determine that manipulation no longer has value as a means for relating. Control destroys all the dignity of any relationship. It dehumanizes the person being held in check.

Perhaps the time has come for you to search around your home to see if it is sheltering a missing person. It could be that if you look over your shoulder you might find him living within your shadow. If you find such a person, you may have to come to terms with the reality that he is there because you put him there by shoving aside his distinctions and discounting his worth. By means of control and intimidation you've kept him there in "his" place.

A Word on Acceptance

Each of us longs for acceptance, though there are many of us who have had to learn to survive without it in one kind of relationship or another. Somewhere, each of us needs to experience the joy of seeing our distinctions rise to the surface and produce a warming effect on others' lives. We need to see that what we are is appreciated, even sought after. Why not at home, and in our marriage? We must see it happening here more than anywhere else. And you know what? Our kids are waiting to see us live this kind of an example before their eyes. If we live it, then most likely they can imitate it when it comes time for them to shelter a mate in their own heart.

If we will learn to acknowledge and accept the whole spectrum of our husband's or wife's distinctions, he or she will settle more quickly into his God-given identity and be able to complement our life the way God intended. Let's put it this way: You accept the me God designed; then my job of accepting myself is made easier. Then as a natural response, I will want to satisfy your needs freely and joyfully, and you'll find us both happier!

Now, it isn't a matter of acceptance alone—expressed appreciation must accompany acknowledgment. Here's what most every mate needs to know: "I'm not just another you, but I am a full-bodied personality who is permitted to bring to you a whole new set of traits you can't afford to be without." Really, each of us needs to know that everything we have to offer is invaluable to the other party. Otherwise, we feel discounted. Frequently we need to say the words that show we both need and appreciate each other's insights, discoveries, opinions, and proposals, and that without them we could not make those broad brush-stroke decisions which have to be made in a world like ours.

Okay, with all that said, take great care in thinking through this question: Could I live comfortably if I was forced to trade places with my mate at this moment? Would I feel trapped? Would I find myself occupying a home in which I felt no worth or citizenship? Tough questions, perhaps. But you need to answer them if you want to create the kind of home where both of you can reach your full potential.

When Trait-Change Is Necessary

When change is needed in our traits and personalities, it is only in the realm of the man-inspired, man-prompted characteristics. Those that are God-given do not need touching up. They are fine the way they are. They only need to be acknowledged and appreciated. However, in the man-related realm when there are characteristics that should be reworked because of the harmful effect they're having on the marriage, exercise great care in the way you handle change.

One man I got to know like a brother used to try to change his wife's offensive traits simply by pointing them out, then telling her she needed to change to demonstrate her love for and submission to him. He in essence used the Bible as leverage to change her to suit himself. Time changed his heart. In fact, as he began taking God seriously, he caught a whole new understanding of marital dignity and began relating to his wife differently. I observed a change in him first and later in her, and I saw how the following pattern helped them overcome the very thing we've been talking about. This process protected their dignity and drew their hearts alongside each other. Let's summarize the process that worked for them in terms you can apply to your own relationship if you need help in this realm.

When one of you feels, or let's say "believes," some type of change is needed in your mate, nagging, manipulation by guilt, belittlement, or harassment will not achieve a healthy result. These will instead produce tension, frustration, and distance at best. To encourage changes, you must *first* express a carefully thought-through concern. *Second*, you must allow adequate time for your concern to be taken in and evaluated by your partner. After all, situations of this sort intimidate the one upon whom the spotlight rests. *Third*, talking further with your mate, hear his reaction to what you have shared to see if your burden is still warranted. Maybe his defense will change your thinking, and you need to be open to change yourself. *Fourth*, offer your full and frequent encouragement until the change is achieved. Then when it is—possibly months, even a year or so later— celebrate!

A word to the caring: If you are the mate who stands opposite the one who needs to change, keep in mind that once you've offered your observations and opinions, then you need to pull back and give your mate space to think and God time to work. Stay out of the way. Also, be aware that if your husband or wife decides the change you suggest is necessary, he might not invite you to assist in that change. Instead, he may seek out a pastor, counselor, or another friend who has been a substantial encouragement to him in past personal battles. *That's okay!* Don't interpret that as a sign of rejection.

But if your mate does ask you for help, be sure you accept his invitation with grace. Guard your motives; don't take unfair advantage to manipulate the change that best suits you and your own distinctions. Love requires the best for both, not for one. Both must win in a marriage. If they don't, then the growth process has been circumvented.

Do you stand on the side where some change is required? If so, work diligently to accept you husband's or wife's observations of you. Listen carefully. Observations—like feelings—aren't necessarily right or wrong. They are simply real. Again, listen carefully to your partner . . . even when the words seem clothed in tension and hostility. Fight back the defensiveness that makes you want to speak prematurely to protect yourself. Always try to hear beyond the words to see if you can pick up the well-intended messages. Don't pay so much attention to vocabulary. It's the intentions of the heart that are far more significant.

Finally, a word to you who must often get your own way. If those close to you do not feel you accept them (even if you think you are doing a good job showing that you do), they feel something is wrong with the way they are put together—either their characteristics and traits that are God-given or those that are man-given. Now, even though they may be wired just right, your lack of expressed acceptance will make them feel like something is really wrong. Then because they love you and want to please you, they start making unnatural changes to spark your acceptance and happiness when in fact nothing needed fixing in the first place. Avoid such a scenario, for it is just as easy to destroy what is beautiful by withholding compliment and affirmation as it is to physically abuse it. Pay close attention to this realm of your relationship.

Shedding Control and Allowing Distinctions to Temper Your Union

Let's return to David's psalm. Remember, it began with a personal evaluation. And it ends the same way:

> Search me, O God, and know my heart;
> Try me and know my anxious thoughts;
> And see if there be any hurtful way in me,
> And lead me in the everlasting way (Psalm 139:23-24).

In the beginning of Psalm 139, David drew our attention to the manner by which God had searched and known him. Now at the end, David allows us to see him as God sees him, to take a fresh look at his heart, his thoughts, and his hurtful ways. Why did he do that? Because he wanted the deity who loved him to call to mind any injurious tendencies he possessed. The heart of this great king was open . . . transparent. He wanted anything about him that could produce pain, loss, trouble, or destruction—for himself or others—to be spotlighted so it could be dealt with and changed. He was highly motivated. He was not content to go on through life sheltering ways that were barriers to his growth and relationships.

How about you? Let's keep it personal. Do you always demand that things go your way? Has your mate altered more of his distinctions for you than you have for him? Does such an imbalance add up to a control which shouldn't have been in your relationship to begin with? Are you really committed to preserving your spouse's distinctions to the same extent you want yours to be protected?

Please keep in mind that acknowledgment, acceptance, and appreciation fully open the door for our distinctions to come out into the open. There they can freely sing and dance together, bringing vitality and beauty to our lives and loves. What's more, *tempering can take place!* In other words, the unrestricted intermingling of our lives makes our marriages suitable, desirable, and balanced because our distinctions have been allowed to blend. And our unions will develop the proper consistency and resilience to better withstand the pressures we increasingly face throughout our years together. That's what tempering is all about. Control and tempering can't exist side by side.

How can such tempering occur in your relationship? How can you show full respect for each other's distinctions? The following process will permit growth and tempering to take place simultaneously:

- Search out and identify each other's distinctions.
- Acknowledge both their existence and origins.
- Work to sincerely understand the importance the other person ascribes to his own traits.
- Mutually pledge to nurture and preserve each other's distinctions in their original form.
- Verbally express recognition and appreciation for what those qualities add to your life.
- Then when necessary, ask forgiveness when you endanger those distinctions, and renew your pledge to protect them and hold them in safekeeping.

When you diligently try to be faithful to this process, you will ensure growth in your friendship, your romance, and your marriage. You will establish the true home your souls both long to have. The resulting harmony and unity will allow the two of you to better face the unavoidable episodes of pain and suffering and disappointment *together* . . . on the same side of the struggle.

Reflection

Several approaches, opinions, or preferences can coexist within a marriage. However, those who've been accustomed to having full control have a difficult time accepting this truth.

The most dominant mate normally wins out when two viewpoints clash. The one who is neither a competent fighter nor an orator withdraws and eventually loses his or her identity.

One of marriage's greatest tragedies occurs when a selfish and strong-handed husband buries the personality and character of his spouse under the guise of so called "biblical" submission.

True love requires mutual respect and mutual submission. Within Scripture that model is clearly seen in the relationship of God the Father to his Son Jesus Christ.

If love, friendship, and romance are to flourish, then dominance and control must be shoved aside. Full recognition of each other's distinctions must be acknowledged.

Steps for Marital Growth

- Search out and identify each other's distinctions.
- Acknowledge both their existence and origins.
- Work to sincerely understand the importance the other person ascribes to his own traits.
- Mutually pledge to nurture and preserve each other's distinctions in their original form.
- Verbally express recognition and appreciation for what those qualities add to your life. If necessary ask forgiveness when you endanger those distinctions, and renew your pledge to protect them and hold them in safekeeping.

Take time now to develop a plan around these steps that will help make your marriage strong and healthy.

8

Trust:

The Primary Ingredient for Security

An ancient observer put it well when he said,
Trust, like the soul, never returns once it's gone.
(Publius Syrus, Maxims)

More often than not, the ancient observer is right. However, to be more accurate, I think I'd say that once trust is lost it *seldom* returns. Couples need to see this before they get themselves into trouble by neglecting or mismanaging trust. But sad to say, too many take the matter seriously only when the lights have dimmed in the realm of their security . . . when the injuries are grave and healing seems questionable.

Perhaps the reason this has been so impressed upon me of late is that I have watched a good number of couples surrounding me lose once-good relationships because they handled trust as if it were a commodity in surplus. Trust is one of those items in your marriage you can take for granted until its absence is acutely felt.

In listening to trustless individuals tell of their experiences, I've found that their trust did not drain away noticeably Instead it faded slowly. Its deterioration was gradual, almost imperceptible to the heart's eye. It subtly blurred before turning to blindness—the same as our eyesight eludes us with aging. But though we can live without eyesight, we can't without trust, especially in our love-friendships and romances. It's vital to our existence and growth.

The Varied Highways of Trust

Over time, Candee and I have come to the conclusion that trust travels any one of four different highways, each of which is dependent upon a couple's history and the choices they make or neglect making. The following histories lived out by four couples Candee and I have known illustrates the patterns of trust we have seen.

Jack and Pauline formed their union nearly a dozen years ago. They had an enjoyable courtship which seemed complete with trust. As the years passed, their friendship grew and led to marriage. Several years into that marriage Jack looked back on his life and realized that he had married young; he saw other men around him in his business setting who were free-spirited around other women. So, wondering if he was being too restrained, he loosened up a bit and began a little mild flirting: "Nothing serious, just fun—it wasn't hurting anyone."

That's when the trust he'd taken for granted in their relationship began to diminish. Pauline saw Jack's flirting and realized what could ultimately happen. Jack took her concern as nagging and began to emotionally park at a distance from her. As he stepped away from her, he stepped toward others who weren't, in his words, "so uptight."

Subtle as the flirting spree seemed, it began a cooling trend in their trust that today has led to a freeze. His flirtation brought him to a near-collision with an affair. Though he terminated the encounter, the trust has remained in deep freeze because Jack has yet to take the steps to rebuild the long-term trust which they both so desperately need. Though physically together, their hearts are rooms apart—enough to keep their marriage empty and threatening.

Jack and Pauline started with trust, but today are without it.

By contrast, Marty and Eileen met while married to other partners. In spite of the fact they'd ripped apart their previous unions, they didn't want their new bond to be sabotaged by an outsider. Though they both needed trust in order to feel secure, they couldn't establish it because of their joint history. Since they remained employed in the same field where they met, jealousy prevailed and trust could not be established.

About fifteen years into their tense, deteriorating marriage, both Marty and Eileen established a personal walk with Jesus Christ. In the wake of the profound change Christ brought to their lives, they looked back upon the past with regret, but realized it couldn't be undone. Yet much to their surprise, a calm came across their relationship because trust had begun to grow. Each realized that the same God they'd both come to trust now wanted to help them to trust each other in turn. And in his energy and love they did just that. They witnessed a miraculous overhaul of a marriage that was poor from the beginning.

Whereas Jack and Pauline's marriage had gone from trust to distrust, Marty and Eileen experienced just the opposite. They began with distrust and today are experiencing a newfound faith in each other.

The sensational part of watching some marriages has been seeing them begin with trust and end the same way. Our good friends Ralph and Mary Ann have such a relationship. They met forty-five years ago, experienced the normal mix of crises couples face, and then some which put their love and Ralph's fidelity to the test—particularly a prolonged sickness that put Mary Ann to bed for more than a year. Then a more-than-usual season of pain touched their life together, the kind that often tears two hearts apart.

Four decades later, this magnificent couple—because of determination—has survived with a compelling love and a well-secured trust. "Why?" you ask them. "Because our trust for one another was highly treasured and aggressively held between us."

Ralph and Mary Ann started with trust and are winding down their lives with a deeper trust.

Perhaps the most exciting situation Candee and I have observed has involved Paul and Sharon. To know them is to love them. They are committed to God, and they are determined to do what is right and nothing else. You'll see what we mean as we tell their story.

Sharon married when she was a teenager. That marriage died. When she met Paul, she still had little understanding of what marriage meant. However, they entered wedlock. She did trust Paul more than she had trusted anyone before. But in a siege of chaos, fear poked through the planks of their immature relationship. Neither was a Christian, so at the time they didn't know the experience of having God check their rude and ugly speech patterns.

While tromping all over what little trust remained, they said many regrettable things . . . things that hurt and refused to be forgotten. With their love and trust dead, they divorced.

This young woman in her mid-twenties began slugging it out as a single parent. Her life was hard. She felt alone and bruised. Her just-departed husband went away, equally alone and wounded. Then much to their surprise, God touched their lives within months of each other. As they began to experience a freshly acquired trust for God, they independently wondered if it were possible to implant that very trust in the mangled marriage affair they'd let die.

Somehow they made contact, explored the risks of trying it once more, and decided—with much fear—to start over. They soon realized the same individuals of the past, with the same ugly and unpolished edges, had reunited. But this time they had a new foundation for bearing with each other which had been unknown to them the first time around.

Today they are succeeding! Their love is growing upon a solid cushion of God-made trust. In fact, though they don't feel their union is unique, others about them sense something special.

Paul and Sharon have an inspirational love that once possessed trust, lost it, then regained it for the long haul of their life together.

Certainly I have no idea which couple you identify with the most. But if you are on trust's downside, then I hope the following thoughts will give you the new sense that your trust can be salvaged regardless of how bad you've been hurt . . . even scarred.

Short-Term Versus Long-Term Trust

The majority of relationships I have noticed have started out relatively trusting. In the early moments of a marriage, trust seems to come fairly automatically. In fact, as I have already said, most don't think about it much until their trust slips away and eludes them. This initial trust is so natural that it is taken for granted. It wasn't hard to come by.

During courtship, two people enjoy being together and having fun, and they're unaware of what is really taking place between them. All they usually think about is that they feel good and at home in each other's presence. But few seem to think about *why*. They don't pay much attention to the role trust has already played in their good feelings and in the formation of their initial friendship.

One of the reasons trust is reasonably automatic is that young, unseasoned couples have had little or no history of injury with each other. They are not yet black and blue. Think about that. Wasn't that relatively true for you?

By comparison, long-term trust is no longer so automatic, particularly when in the course of time those things surface in human nature that wound and upset the balance of the human heart. Some time after the wedding, mature trust becomes the product of careful and thoughtful nurturing, and only that!

What happens is this: A husband and wife flow along reasonably well with each other. They are comfortable until one of them does something that inserts a splinter into their trust. It might be an unkind word, an ill-timed jab made in public, a prolonged and unexplained silence, or a series of late arrivals home without good and verifiable reasons. Splinters also come in the form of rudeness, thoughtlessness, accusation, inappropriate anger, inaccountability, or rough treatment—emotional or physical.

You see, once a splinter festers and becomes surrounded by infection and inflammation, the trust becomes either tender or brittle. The longer it's left uncared for, the more acute the problem grows. When impaired, trust is neglected for months—then years—and the relationship turns painful, perhaps untouchable.

Most of us have experienced that to one extent or another. And I might add as an important side note that splinters are not always implanted by heartless disregard. Sometimes they are the result of ignorance. Just the same, disregard and ignorance alike hurt and endanger the trust-base of an enduring friendship, romance, and marriage.

A Close-up on Trust

Generally speaking, couples are not in the process of trust-building so much as they are trust-rebuilding. As I have already said, trust seems to prevail effortlessly in the preliminary days of most marriages and is taken for granted until it is threatened, damaged, or destroyed; then it must be restored or replaced by a faith that is more realistic and resilient.

Trust is a firm belief or confidence we have in the honesty, integrity, reliability, and justice of one to whom we're related. It's also the foundation upon which a close bond rests which allows both individuals to grow and fail, to disclose their pasts and explore their shared future.

From my point of view, refined by the experience of my own marriage, I see trust as the atmosphere of assurance in a union that says, "I feel with you that I am both appreciated and safe, and that you will not mishandle my body or my soul; I know that you won't discount or write off my concerns . . . and that you'll love me at least as well as you love yourself."

The act of trusting is placing our thoughts and feelings in someone else's care—someone who is ready to receive them and take on the responsibility of sheltering them.

My own experience with trust shows me at least two things:

It serves as the *catalyst* that keeps on encouraging Candee and me out and into the open where our hearts can continue to grow together in love.

And it provides us the *tranquilizer* our marriage needs to calm our most natural fears of being hurt or used.

Trust-Splintering Elements

What about the specific circumstances that fatigue trust? As I've said, trust doesn't leave a heart immediately, unless perhaps infidelity crashes into a life. Trust is usually worn away gradually. Here's a list of some of those erosive elements I've identified:

- Marital separations (which seldom make sense except when there is physical abuse)
- The consistent failure to be where you said you'd be
- Coming home late continuously without good reason
- Withholding information, or sharing it partially at best
- Permitting jealousy to run unchecked
- Holding back words and gestures of affirmation
- A wandering eye
- Lack of expressed appreciation or statements of worth
- Lying—even in its subtler forms
- Unaccountability
- Irresponsibility
- Flirting (which incidentally is usually as destructive to a marriage as is a well-staged affair)

The items above all appear to be just what they are: negative. Yet there's one I have saved till now which on the surface seems to some to be a strength, and that is *peacemaking.* Peacemakers tend to fall back on Jesus' words from his sermon on the mountain: "Blessed are the peacemakers, for they shall be called sons of God" (Matthew 5:9).

However, the context of his address wasn't marriage, nor was he saying that one should remain silent while another walks all over him. Peacemaking is not the withholding of opinion or truth in order to have calm at all costs. Yet that's what happens in many marriages. One or both holds back the truth for fear of getting into a fight.

This was the case with Don and Andrea, whose relationship appeared outwardly quiet. At home, however, it was tense. You couldn't stop the hemorrhage in either one's heart.

Don and Andrea had taken up peacemaking. They would do anything to avoid conflict. Andrea was having problems with her weight and Don didn't like it. Apart from gently encouraging her on occasion, he lugged around his ill feelings. When it got to the point he couldn't handle it, however, he would get angry—but always over peripheral issues. He didn't want to hurt her, so he'd always gloss over the real issue and light on ones she'd get over quickly.

I remember one time when he bought a camera, knowing she'd be upset. They had the money, so he knew that wasn't the issue. But he was well aware that she thought a camera—the kind he liked—was but a grown man's toy. The day came when he couldn't resist. He bought the camera. But to keep peace he kept the purchase secret. As always, she found out via the kids. She got upset. Why? Because she wondered again, "What else are you hiding from me? If you can't be honest about a camera, you certainly won't be honest about more serious things."

At the same time he was trying to quiet tensions, he was actually adding to the erosion of her trust in him. This peacemaking pattern was not unique to him. She worked it as well, but in other ways.

Andrea's close friend was involved in an extramarital affair. This friend frequently confided in her, telling her everything that was going on in the relationship. In fact, Andrea was often told more than she wanted to know, but because she was a peacemaker, she didn't know how to tell her friend she'd had enough. Andrea found herself in an awkward position because she was good friends with her girlfriend's husband as well. Don became aware of the whole scene.

When Andrea came to me for counsel regarding her own inability to trust Don, we got into the matters that prompted her concerns—one of which was the camera incident. However, in the course of our conversation this situation with her girlfriend's affair surfaced. As she explained it to me, I asked her what she would do if her friend's husband came to her and asked if she knew of anything that was going on between his wife and someone else. She replied before I could finish my question, "I'd lie to him and say I knew nothing because I wouldn't want him to get mad at me." Next I asked, "Don knows that doesn't he? What do you think that is saying to him?" Following a long pause, she responded, "That if I'd be willing to hide information regarding someone else's affair from her mate, then what might I possibly be hiding about my own life from him?"

And that's exactly what Don was thinking. Each was hiding information to keep the other from getting angry. And because of their "peacemaking tendencies," each was killing the very trust they needed to share between themselves.

Another couple we met with suffered from a similar problem. Bob and Helen's scene was painful, yet common. In the counseling process, Helen began talking honestly with me about the state of her own heart as Bob listened in. This woman, nearly fifty, was starting to be truly honest with a husband she had feared for more than twenty years. Bob was probably the most interested person present as he heard things he had never before been told. In fact, many others had heard from Helen what he was now hearing for the first time.

Helen labored through every sentence, hand-selecting each word and apologizing for every declaration. She'd been afraid of Bob for years, afraid he'd lose control. Truth is that he had gotten to the point where his frustration had peaked because he seldom knew what she really felt. But she had contributed to the very situation she had grown to despise.

Be it peacemaking, flirting, irresponsibility, or any other of the items listed—none can be tolerated if a healthy, trusting relationship is going to work. They've got to be seen for what they are: destructive and erosive.

The Link Between Trust and Demonstration

Contained in the New Testament is a statement on trust (or faith) which specifically applies to man's relationship to God, but can also apply in a more general sense to human relationships. The statement is this:

> Faith is the assurance of things hoped for, the conviction of things not seen (Hebrews 11:1).

In the King James translation it reads:

> Faith is the substance of things hoped for, the evidence of things not seen.

Assurance, conviction, substance, evidence—those are the critical words that foster or constitute this precious commodity in a marriage.

Let's think about a couple of these terms a minute and personalize them. Try to see where they fit your own union.

Basically, *assurance, substance,* and *fulfillment* are the same thing dressed in different letters. People enter relationships particularly because they hope for certain kinds of fulfillment. When coming to God, for example, we long to have our emptiness eradicated, our sins forgiven, and our future secured by him. In the relationship we begin with him we exercise trust that he will fulfill all those and more. If we had any idea that he couldn't or wouldn't, we would quickly withdraw from him. We would not place ourselves in his care. Instead, we would pull away with suspicion or fear.

When entering marriage, we in essence do the same thing. We give ourselves to each other because we believe we have all the assurances that we will be well cared for, as we desire. And trust works until those assurances are undermined or the substances of hope dry up. We want our legitimate desires fulfilled in an intimate relationship. But the moment we question our partner's capacity to fulfill our God-given needs, our trust is immediately threatened. *Assurance* and *substance* are bywords of trust we just can't disregard.

The word *evidence* is equally important. Trust responds to

evidence and demonstration. The more a husband or wife shows loving actions that validate love-words, the more trust has to feed and thrive on. A major source of conflict in many marriages, however, involves the opposite. The words are present, but corresponding actions are extinct. That's often the way it is with kids as well. They are told they are loved, but the short-circuiting of loving acts and loving moments immediately devalues their parents' claims.

Candee and I look at trust and all that goes with it as a delicate piece of fine china. Its beauty seems to grow with time, as does its value. Therefore, as we move through life we pay careful attention to how we handle it. In our own marriage, we are aiming our sights beyond our own relationship to our children. And the trust we're working on preserving today will be an heirloom that will be handed down to them tomorrow to be enjoyed and observed in their own unions. We want to give them something to imitate.

Creating the Environment for Trust Rebuilding

Both the preservation of trust and the rebuilding of trust require the same kinds of environments, the same controlled conditions. Here's briefly what I see those to be: *Full disclosure.* Though some argue that damage is done by complete disclosure, I argue the opposite. When couples disclose everything and keep the information free flowing, there is an inaudible assurance that says, "You are not going to be surprised; you are not about to be devastated." That's not to say every detail needs to be disclosed, but the core of past-life involvements and episodes should be revealed.

Case in point. Two couples I've counseled in the past have tough histories, particularly the kind that tend to threaten trust. In both instances the husbands trafficked in homosexuality while in their young single adult years. After seeking God's help for repatterning of unnatural desires, each experienced a new appreciation for the love of one from the opposite sex. When those relationships took on serious overtones, each man came to me and asked, "What do I do about my past? Bury or reveal it?

If I tell her about this now, won't she be devastated and her love and trust for me be destroyed?"

In both instances I advised them, just as I have done with others to reveal their misspent past with full candor and let the other one have the privilege of dealing with the information. I told them that more than likely, if they didn't learn of it now, they would discover it in years to come. Trust would suffer more then than it would now. So when the time was right, each ran the risk of disclosure.

To their surprise, each feminine counterpart not only accepted the information, but confessed an even deeper bond because full disclosure was made. The fact is, each woman felt that the discipline demonstrated through change and the subsequent ongoing victory over the past lifestyle was enough to authenticate her man's trustworthiness.

The beauty in one of those two instances is that the woman confessed in turn her own heterosexual compromise and told how God had worked in her to bring about change as well. She assured him that she saw his compromise to be no worse than hers.

Both couples chose to marry, each appreciating that the later emergence of any surprise or threatening information would not one day disrupt the relationship God had orchestrated. I am pleased to tell you that at this moment each couple is happily married and secure in their love. Why? Because full disclosure led to the curing of their trusts.

Generous words. Another condition for encouraging trust is dialogue. Human love needs an interchange of hearts. Words are important. As I look back on my own union, I can see how dialogue has caused our souls to rest beside each other . . . for thousands of hours of open talk.

Many couples I've encountered in crises quit talking or significantly reduced expressing their thoughts and feelings, their dreams and imaginations. In the absence of words arose suspicions—and most frequently unfounded! But just the same, they seemed real. Suspicions are like wildfire: They can burn across the landscape of trust with the speed of a fast-driving wind.

Words supply information. Information gives the heart a basis for trust. Trust calms the soul. But a lack of words can short out the whole cycle.

Devoted eyes. The eyes are sometimes more skilled communicators than mouths. They tell all and hide nothing. I've listened to many mates describe the confusing messages their husband's or wife's eyes gave them while looking at others. One wife in particular said that she longed to have her husband look at her in the same way he sized up others. When a husband's or wife's eye roves, it undoes any sense of security their marriage could enjoy.

Gracious speech. One cannot trust someone who is gruff and tense or rude and nasty. But as I mentioned several chapters ago, many times a person shows more kindness to a stranger than to his mate. The art of gracious words has been lost on all fronts—marriage included. This seems particularly true in big cities, where folks have to fight to survive, where people are in a hurry and where they live crammed tightly together, with no space and hardly any solitude. And in that world productivity and competition prevail. In this arena are pressures that can easily be submitted to. But marriages can't survive in such shadows. The beauty of a home is that these shadows can be lit up and chased away by love and kindness. A home can be made a sanctuary where souls are preserved in graciousness and where talk can be dispensed in gentility to those God has entrusted to one's care.

With all this in mind, what are the steps we can take to solidify or rebuild a trust?

Building a Lord-based Rather Than a Land-based Trust

I believe that if you pay close attention to the following seven steps of trust construction, or a combination of them suited to you at this time, you will soon witness a deepening of security in your marriage. Of course, there is no magic in any one step, because actually each requires first a choice and second, hard work. Keep that in mind as you look at each one.

Step one: *First trust God for one another's benefit.* When

we place our trust in God and experience him fully, we gain insights into trust that would otherwise be beyond our reach. For the most part we see from him what we should be doing and what we could be doing to engender trust in others.

For example, not only does he survive the garbage and insensitivity we express to him, he also remains constant in his commitment to us. The words he expresses to us, we must learn to echo diligently to our mate:

> I will never fail you nor forsake you. . . . No one shall pluck you out of my hand.
>
> (Words paraphrased from Joshua 1:5 and John 10:28)

A little bit of reflection shows us that it's not our trust in him that activates his commitment to us. It's the other way around: His commitment and his love already demonstrate to us a reason to trust him. It is that quality about him we need to import into our relationships. What he has shown toward us causes us to feel that with him we are safe. So by trusting him, we come into contact with a model we all need to emulate.

Trust in God also gives a stability to our lives which in turn makes another person comfortable in our presence. Jeremiah, God's prophet, recorded these words:

> Blessed is the man who trusts in the LORD
> And whose trust is the LORD.
> For he will be like a tree planted by the water,
> That extends its roots by a stream
> And will not fear when the heat comes;
> But its leaves will be green,
> And it will not be anxious in a year of drought
> Nor cease to yield fruit.
> (Jeremiah 17:7-8)

I read those words and here are some of the things I see: Trust in the Lord establishes a setting for survival; it makes possible the elimination of fear; trust produces a soul-comfort in tough times; and trust allows growth to continue in the face of crisis.

Step two: *Guard your self-discipline for each other's security.* A husband or wife will not be able to deposit trust in a bank that is not well-guarded. By that I mean that when husbands and wives do not see their mates taking charge of themselves, their disciplines, and their living patterns—sexually, spiritually, attitudinally, emotionally, financially—they are not easily going to place themselves into that person's care. We could express it this way:

> If I know I can trust you to be responsible with all realms of your own life, my trust for you is made easier . . . the roadblocks are removed. But if you can't be responsible in taking charge of yourself, then how are you going to be responsible with me?

That's the idea.

Step three: *Develop trust for the sake of each other's confidence.* Isaiah 12:2 helps us to understand that decided trust dispels fear. The prophet wrote these words as he described the renewed relationship Israel would one day have with God and what she would say in return:

> Behold, God is my salvation,
> I will trust and not be afraid.

Note the connection here between trust and fear. Israel purposes trust, and as a result, fear is unraveled. You see, what works in an intimate relationship with God is applicable also to an intimate relationship with a mate.

We appreciate what Isaiah records in the remainder of that verse:

> For the Lord God is my strength and song,
> And He has become my salvation.

That's what trust produces: strength, joy, and security. Trust in a trustworthy God does that in an eternal sense, and trust in a trustworthy mate produces that in a temporal sense. It all adds up to a necessary confidence we need for the backbone of our living together.

Step four: *Handle each other with care and respect.* By this I mean that in all you do, seek to do each other good; act in behalf of your friend and mate's best interest while aiming to avoid injury.

A wise mother of an ancient king alerted him to the kind of wife which his search should uncover. King Lemuel's mom first asked this question:

> An excellent wife, who can find?

Then she implanted these thoughts in her son's thinking:

> The heart of her husband trusts in her. . . .
> She does him good and not evil
> All the days of her life.
> (Proverbs 31:10-12)

More than likely she changed gender terms when giving the counsel to her daughter while she was in search of a husband. The essence of her counsel was simple: You can trust one you know has determined to do you good. That means joint, careful handling of all dimensions of each other's lives.

Step five: *Establish and preserve your eye contact.* Here is something Candee and I have begun doing which has enhanced the tenderness we feel toward each other: We have begun praying while looking into each other's eyes. Believe us, it is not distracting, as you might think. Actually, we have found ourselves in tears on occasion with a new sense of soul-bond, and we have quietly laughed, feeling a deeper sense of freshness and vitality. It was scary at first, but the scare was offset by the delight our souls experienced.

We were first introduced to this thought at a couples' retreat in northern California. In the final hours of the weekend, couples were presented with a musical on marriage. Toward the end of the program, the house lights dimmed. The husbands and wives were then asked to hold hands, look into each other's eyes, and sing, "Oh, I Love You with the Love of the Lord." The initial sense of awkwardness was quickly overruled by a set of emotions similar to the ones we felt the night we exchanged our wedding vows.

What touched the two of us beyond our own feelings was the sight of several couples who'd come to the weekend with plans for divorce . . . ones who had come to the conference as a last-ditch effort to salvage lifeless romances. Tears streamed from their eyes as their souls interlocked through eye contact. Perhaps you need a dose of that yourselves.

Step six: *Allow each other time and space to recover.* Time and familiarity calm our fears and stimulate our trust. Whether the bruises to our trust are incurred by intention or by ignorance, it takes time to recover, and that is normal. The heart is delicate. It doesn't rebound immediately. If we overlook that reality, we will try to hurry up a process that can't afford to be crowded. Fragile items like trust return cautiously when no appearance of threat is near.

Step seven: *Give each other generous assurance . . . it won't spoil.* One cannot trust another until he has the ongoing assurance that his counterpart is resolutely committed to his preservation and welfare. Actually, the beauty of generous assurance is that it keeps couples tied tightly together as they struggle jointly through commonly shared crises. And what in turn happens is that when couples struggle together, they remain on the same side of the struggle as two friends in love. Thus their bond tightens yet more. Perhaps, like me, you have discovered that without generous assurance, knots can gradually loosen.

A Personal Appeal

If your trust has come unglued or untied, if it has fallen down around your legs, causing you to stumble as you try to move along, then I ask you to give serious attention to these seven steps or activities of trust building—or rebuilding, as the case may be. If I could reduce this whole chapter to four reminders, it would be these:

> Truth . . . no matter how painful.
> Openness . . . no matter how cumbersome.
> Accountability . . . no matter how inconvenient.
> Grace . . . no matter how awkward.

Reflection

Trust is perhaps the most fragile commodity held within a marriage.

All too often couples only pay attention to the health of trust when it has been severely impaired.

The maintenance of a good trust relationship should be viewed as a daily contract—laborious as it might seem at first.

Mature, long-term trust is the product of careful and thoughtful nurturing. It does not come about by chance.

Without a well-cultivated, well-preserved trust, a marriage will more than likely flounder in time.

Trust provides a marital friendship with the single most important ingredient it needs for security.

Steps for Marital Growth

- Think about the degree of trust in your relationship. Is it strong, relatively good, threatened, or dead? If it is less than strong, what has affected your trust, and how long has that deterioration been taking place?
- Formulate a working definition of trust that best embodies your own ideals. Ask your mate to do the same. Then compare your definitions. What differences are there between the two that should become part of your focus as you work at trust building?

9

Emotion:

The Pathway of Expression for the Heart

One day this past winter, Joe and I spent several hours over lunch. For the past forty years, Joe's life had been the business world. With consummate skill, this controlled gentleman had parlayed a small sum into a full-sized fortune in less than a decade. Joe was most comfortable when talking in terms of projections and roll-overs, and he could put together a deal that was as fine as any exquisite sonata. Listening to his peers, I could tell they were envious of his sixth sense for money growth and management.

His wife Lou was equally pleasant—a fine complement to him. When they were together in the presence of others, he smiled graciously while she carried the conversation for the two of them. He was most content that way.

I wasn't quite sure why we'd gotten together for lunch. I knew it wasn't to talk business. So before the meal was done I decided to take the plunge. I asked Joe, "As you've moved along your career path to where you are today, what are your feelings?

Are you happy with yourself? Have you become what you wanted to be?" I was determined to get to know a bit of his heart.

He wasn't offended with my questions, but his response took me by surprise: "Ed, I'm not sure how to answer those questions. I want to, but I don't know how. No one has ever cultivated that kind of expression in me, and I don't know how to do it on my own."

That was the day it dawned on me that many seemingly emotionless men were anxious to reveal this side of themselves, but had little or no idea where to begin. They were prisoners waiting to be paroled.

All these years this likeable guy had lived handicapped, not knowing how to express his inner feelings to the outside world. Though he was fluent when it came to addressing technical and financial issues, he was a stranger to the language of his own heart. Some of you, both men and women, readily identify with Joe because you're there right now.

Emotional Expression Is a Hot Issue

The subject of emotional expression always seems to stir reaction when raised in a mixed group. The more-often-than-not response comes from wives who begin looking around the room to each other with message-sending eyes that say, "Here's our chance to get our strokes in. Let's not pass it up. Who'll be first?"

Repeatedly I have seen this issue given lopsided treatment, and this is personally offensive to me. I find the subject tends to be treated as if it were primarily a husband-related problem. I have been in groups where wives or husbands have dominated such discussions while their embarrassed and gracious mates listened on as they were run into the ground by their spouses. Each time everyone present lost. Nothing good was gained. No one was challenged and motivated to change. The wounds were merely aggravated.

Though it is true that men are often emotionally restricted or expressively bottled up, I find that women can be as well. Because of this, I have decided to treat this matter as a husband-wife need. I have no intention of making gender-jabs in order to force one or the other into a corner. Yet at times I may direct my comments a specific way because from the wider scope of my experience I feel it is appropriate to do so, and because the mention of it will benefit both mates.

Really Emotionless?

A frequent complaint of unhappy mates is that the one who shares their name is cold, closeted, unexpressive, feelingless, too mechanical or disinterested. And on the surface it may appear that way. But usually the person clothed in that garb does in fact have deep feelings . . . true emotions. Yet for one reason or another, the expression of these emotions is blocked.

What I want to underscore with you is the fact that people are not normally emotionless. Instead, they may be *handicapped* in expressing the things their emotionally expressive counterparts find easy to verbalize and display. In other words, they are not dry by intent; they just don't know the language by which emotions are revealed. They don't know how inside movements are reported to the outside world—to mates and family members—except that they do it with embarrassment and uneasiness.

When individual mates have good emotional expressions early in their relationships, it's usually because they have had good, effective coaching in their growing-up years. Now, most of us didn't have that, so what we've tried on our own has often failed. Understandably! Also, many men and women can't look back to trustworthy models whom they can imitate. So for all practical purposes, they are *expressively handicapped* and not necessarily emotionally dead. One doesn't look too far to find adults still hauling around scars from the battering and abuse received by messed-up parents who ran roughshod over them in their homegrown years.

Thus husbands and wives with such "heritages" have watched on as their emotional displays turned inward where their feelings could find refuge from insensitive outsiders. That's not hard to comprehend. But it is usually overlooked by lonely, hungry, frustrated mates who are finally about to give up.

Years of emotion-sheltering aren't reversed easily. So an anxious mate trying to uncork the one they love can sow destruction by insensitively prying, banging, forcing, or tearing the lid off their mate's expressionless heart. But that's precisely what desperate spouses tend to do.

Good results in this realm of marriage take time to jell. Therefore, the objective must be not to lose heart while a beloved mate is in the tunnel of change.

Good Emotional Expression Is Worth Learning

In the things I am about to say, I will not treat emotions as a clinician would be inclined to do. Neither is my intent to tell you how to manage particular kinds of emotions such as anger, bitterness, guilt, depression, fear, or regret. What I want is to sell you on the thought that good emotional expression is the prerequisite to two-hearted intimacy. Others have done a noteworthy job of handling the management of certain emotions and have written entire books in the process. Thus I point your attention to them for the specifics.

Let's talk intimacy a moment. If your husband or wife doesn't feel that he knows how you feel about a wide variety of issues, he is going to look upon you as a stranger—mild or otherwise. Heart-bonding is circumvented when a spouse lacks acquaintance with this one-third portion of your being. If you are an emotionally unexpressive mate, you must realize the one trying to love you can't get close enough to you by knowing only the realms of your thinking and choosing. In fact, your intellectual side can't compensate for your lack of emotional silence and provide for the other person the warmth and security he needs from you. Emotions can't cover for intellect, and intellect can't be substituted for emotional expression.

If you care seriously about having a full-bodied marriage relationship, then you'll pay close attention to your openness or lack of it. And then you'll seek whatever help is needed to properly posture your emotional displays. You may have to undo the stranger you've become to that one who started out being your friend.

A Profile of Emotion

Our emotions are the movements of our soul. They are the sensations we experience that bear the labels of joy, grief, pain, disillusionment, love, delight, warmth, astonishment, fright. They are the stirrings of our inner persons reflected in our cellular shells. Also, emotions are the subterranean shifts in feeling we encounter that aren't necessarily activated by sight, hearing, taste, or smell—though they may be. These inside movements, stirrings, or sensations may change several times an hour. They may occur in multiples, forming duets and trios that sometimes produce harmony and at other times create dissonance.

My reason for defining emotions is that those who have become emotionally sheltered have usually lost touch with the distinctions between thinking and feeling. So I believe those distinctions are worth restatement.

Emotional expressions get beyond the talk about issues and events and people by themselves—they get down to talking about the inside influence those things have upon us, how we feel our lives are touched by them. Also, emotions differ from intellectual activity, which is basically characterized by deliberation, analysis, evaluation, and reflection. Perhaps I can best put it in perspective this way: *Emotional expression is thinking aloud from the heart instead of the head.*

One husband in Scripture who was attentive to his feelings and willing to express them was David, Israel's second monarch. Reading his psalms, it's not long before you realize David reported his full repertoire of emotions in the lyrics of those pieces.

In one particular song he describes a problem I've seen plague marriages in this century, and though his psalm doesn't speak of his own emotions at this point (nor is he speaking specifically of marriage), he cites a problem that does touch mates. In talking about a friend who betrayed him—one with whom he had once experienced great peace—he said,

> His words were oily smooth, but in his heart was war.
> His words were sweet, but underneath were daggers.
> (Psalm 55:21 TLB)

The editors of the NASB translate the Hebrew text,

> His speech was smoother than butter,
> But his heart was war;
> His words were softer than oil,
> Yet they were drawn swords.

David helps us to see that a full-scale conflict can exist within a person's warring soul unseen by anyone else—including a husband or wife. That's a sad yet common occurrence and often seems to happen because mates fear running the risk of being known, or they have been improperly taught that they should hold it all in.

I have watched different ones live such guarded lives—ones who've been relentlessly careful to bury their flaws and suppress their "weaker" emotions. They have ended up having finely tuned outer shells that look great while hurt and pain drip off the inner lining of their lives. Their words are masterfully smooth, but their hearts are warring with the anger and ache. They keep their cracks patched and painted so no one else can observe them. Happy they look, bound they live. They cry in darkness away from even the sympathetic eyes of the world . . . eyes owned by tender mates, compassionate friends, and vitally interested fellow Christians who could each make a difference.

Some individuals think that strong survivors, capable leadership-type folks, wear their soft feelings on the inside only. This way the people about them will remain assured that that person is truly qualified to remain in control, and that their leadership is worth following.

On the other hand are those who have been taught that the spiritually mature Christian smiles all the time and routinely sets aside his or her real feelings in deference to those they are serving or discipling. Sometimes that may be wise to do, but mates deserve different treatment than that from the one they love. Mates aren't disciples. And they are certainly not constituents. Instead, they are soul-companions, as we mentioned earlier, and they deserve more than a mask of controlled emotion from their husband or their wife.

This kind of person who has gained an unrealistic view even of Christ would have felt awkward in his presence when he cried or expressed disappointment. A common, perverted belief among many Christians is that the mature individual shows no pain, vents no anger, displays no discouragement. They see these disciplines as the varying badges of true godly character.

I think these persons would have been most surprised to see Jesus initially bemoan the death of his friend from Bethany and grieve with Lazarus's sisters before raising him from death. Others of us, however, would have wished to step up and embrace him and have him embrace us in return, knowing that he too could spill tears and allow his loss to be expressed—in front of earthlings, no less.

Actually, both kinds of persons mentioned deny God's creative fiat, which included human emotional expression. And perhaps believing themselves to be strong they've closeted the very displays that act as magnets in drawing other souls alongside. Thus the result is distance, mystery, and an insatiable curiosity. Intimacy can only be bred when two friend-mates jointly remove the lids on their emotions and allow each other to see their soul-stirrings in their unguarded forms.

It's through the expression of emotions that we project our naked souls into each other's lives. And there true intimacy is achieved.

Still One Step Ahead

With all the talk today about the emotional chasm that separates men and women, I have wondered, Why is it that men in general remain expressively handicapped? Why are so many still bottled up and emotionally inhibited?

In most instances I've observed, wives are more familiar with the language of emotion in general than are their husbands, perhaps because women as a whole have valued that side of themselves, thus keeping it alive. They've been coached by moms on how to display their feelings, knowing that if they do so it is not considered a sign of weakness. But men somewhere along the line gained the idea that to display feelings, particularly those which are softer and more sensitive, was a sign of flaw and weakness. Thus for some time men have taught one another, and are still teaching, that a controlled outer appearance is a virtue. However, in many men with whom I have had contact lately, I can see that belief beginning to change—especially as the traditional men's and women's worlds have become more intertwined.

I am finding more and more that men are agreeing they need to learn ways to express themselves. They're struggling with the practical questions, When do I learn this dimension of myself? and Where do I go for help? Women, who are accustomed to displaying their emotions and talking with the language of emotion, can usually turn to one another for comfort, and together they can keep this realm of their lives well exercised. Still, for men it's quite different. In most working environments there's little opportunity for them to develop well-roundedness in their emotional expressions. Weary at day's end, they are not up to going to counseling in the evenings where someone could coach them out of their restraint and into freedom.

Most husbands could learn something about emotional freedom from their wives, but to do so, both would have to be together more often when they're each at their physical and emotional best. I don't think that includes early mornings or late evenings, when one or the other is tired. Candee and I have found that we have had to cultivate our emotional togetherness when we both are alert and receptive to one another. That means during the daylight and early evening hours. Therefore, we've come to see how important the weekends are to us and our growth.

A Word about Weekends

Looking around us, Candee and I have found that couples generally fill up their weekends or days off with things that take the two of them in separate directions. Perhaps the best times for growing together emotionally, enjoying the intermingling of their hearts, are preempted by a host of other things. If your weekends are filled with club meetings, sports, work, and other people, then some changes in priorities are in order. Men can be the worst offenders in this area, and I feel we bear the better brunt of the blame.

You see, these kinds of commitments and activities will not encourage the bonding of our hearts, nor will they enhance the development of our emotional growth, but they can surely keep us distracted from the directions we need to take in our relationships. These kinds of commitments and activities will not wrap their indifferent arms around us in the autumn of our lives and comfort us with warmth and love. They are totally powerless to do so. Become convinced of that before you damage your relationships. Put them in perspective. Keep 'em in balance.

Together seize your weekends. Protect at least some significant portion of them like you would any other valued asset. Then spend the time that's required to develop open, rewarding conversation and emotional growth.

Making sure that you have both the time and setting to grow emotionally is the first priority you must protect, that is, if you want your heart to learn the movements that will draw someone else close to you. The other priority is determining to learn the language of emotion itself.

The Unique Language of Emotion

Mark and his wife have been distant almost from the beginning of their marriage. Somehow the two of them survived two decades of tough married life. Her chief complaint was that he would never let her into his heart. The only emotional expression he knew was gruffness. Either he was gruff or he was quiet—there were no in-betweens.

Realizing his life was empty, he came to talk to me, wondering, What can you do to energize a relationship? It soon became apparent that Mark was gruff by nature. He didn't feel gruff, but he'd grown up in that kind of an environment and it felt normal to him. Meredith was made uncomfortable by it. His gruffness kept her at arm's length for years, yet she still wanted to get in and alongside him.

The first thing I communicated to Mark was that if he'd be willing to cultivate his emotional displays and expressions and learn the language of emotion which went beyond his gruffness, that he would soon find his heart full and he would see Meredith warming up to him. The first thing he said was, "That sounds so foreign to me, and I'm not even sure what you mean. But if you think it will work, I'll take the risk."

Seeing that Meredith knew the language of the heart, at my prompting he began asking her questions: "If I were to try to convey to you what I think I'm feeling in this particular area, what kinds of words would you use, and how would you go about doing it?" She began telling him how she would handle various situations he described. She gave him some hints on how she thought he could reroute his reactions around those responses that would normally devastate her.

One late afternoon he came by and said, "Ed, I am frightened. I am doing the things Meredith is suggesting, and they are working. But they feel so peculiar. I just hope I can hang in there." He did hang in there. Today, Mark has rounded a corner of his life and he'll never be the same, nor will his marriage.

Communicating almost anything depends upon having some way to convey it. Going into foreign countries, no matter how beautiful they are, is difficult if the traveler doesn't know the language that will help him or her negotiate inns or transportation or read menus. Knowing the language makes for a more pleasant journey.

What happened to Mark? He learned that within the province of a relationship, emotional expression has a language all its own. And it must be learned if the two people inside the relationship are going to travel and survive together.

John Stuart Mill, the English philosopher of the mid-to-late 1800s, termed language "the light of the mind." What Mark learned was that *the language of emotion is the light of the heart*. Put another way, the language of emotion is the tongue and speech of the soul.

People must let themselves go and talk about the stirrings they feel within them in order to converse in that fashion. And yes, it can be frightening or awkward at first, but the longterm result is fulfilling.

All Expression Need Not Be the Same

Healthy marriages allow for bilingual expression. That is, the style of expression for one mate may vary somewhat from the other. They need not be identical, and probably won't be. Meredith is having to learn that now. She has had to realize that Mark's first expressions were similar to hers only because he was allowing himself to funnel his feelings through her words and phrases. But the more he has come to feel comfortable with this aspect of himself, the more he has run with his own heart and given out his expressions through the vehicle of his own inclinations.

Growing mates realize in time that the style of expression is not nearly so important as the fact that some kind of expression is attempted. And then each has to determine to accept his mate's soul-speech for what it is in its own original form.

In light of this, I must say that wives—because of being generally more adept at good expression—have tended to set their patterns up as the norm. And often this has blocked the growth process. When their men have tried to step into this foreign territory, their wives have called their attempts "fouls" because they haven't matched the patterns they've best understood.

Some of you have a mate like this who is still waiting for you to acknowledge the only dialect they know. My encouragement is this: Study your mate's expressions in light of his past influences and experiences. Then cultivate a willingness to accept his most recent attempts for what they are. Don't discount them. Whether you're a husband or a wife married to a partner who's been expressively handicapped in the past, allow your mate time to develop. Accept his attempts more at heart value than at face value. Work to be as patient with his growth process as you would be with a child learning these same things for the first time.

Surprise! In the Beginning There May Be Strain

Of course, disclosure comes hard for those unaccustomed to showing their feelings. But that same disclosure can put an unexpected strain on the mate who is listening to it for the first time.

When Al and Lynda first entered this process, they found this to be true, especially Lynda. When they married eight years ago, Lynda enjoyed being around Al. He was easy going and had a fabulous sense of humor.

He was gracious to Lynda, but unexpressive. Lynda treasured the peace and harmony they had. But she realized six years into their marriage that Al was still a stranger. She didn't know how he felt about much of anything. She was simply laughing her way through life with a man she hardly knew. Most of his emotions were fenced up beyond her reach.

Lynda asked Al to attend Marriage Encounter, thinking that it might help to open him up. Open him up it did! For forty-eight hours Al talked almost non-stop because something someone said that weekend clicked. It was as if he'd found a new toy to play with. She wasn't ready to handle the flood of unplugged emotions and actually found herself overcome by the deluge. She finally said, "Hold it! I can't take any more right now." She just needed time to adjust to what was happening to him . . . and to her.

I tell you this because some of you reading these words right now may desperately want your mate to open up and draw you in, but you must be prepared. Along with the disclosure may come a temporary discomfort, particularly at first. Tolerate it in the transitionary days if you want growth to continue.

For Those Married to an Expressively Handicapped Spouse

Though you are anxious to know what's going on in the subterranean realms of your husband or wife, avoid accusation and blame. Remember, generally people are not expressively handicapped because they choose to be. They are that way because of molding that took place somewhere in their life. If you want them to gain freedom, getting on their case won't help to release them. It will only place them on the defensive and strengthen their resistance to you.

When you sense your mate is trying to open up, leave well enough alone. Listen and learn to appreciate his most primitive attempts. Accept what he has to offer for the moment and don't show disappointment if the extent of his expression falls shy of what you had hoped for.

Be prepared to ask questions, and do so gently. You'll know immediately when you've asked too much. If that happens, don't submit to feelings of anxiety, but quietly ask God to cushion your own emotional reaction so it won't turn to anger, hurt, or frustration. Remember, the journey of the soul from the closet into the open takes time and is achieved by degrees—sometimes minute ones.

Periodically, tell your mate what his efforts mean to you. Let him know specifically what it is doing for your own well-being. Without overdoing it, help him to understand this is just what you have needed.

Hold back the tendency to orchestrate your mate's expressive development. There's a fine line between support and coaching. Though you will have to find that line for yourself, don't be overactive in the process.

Pray for your mate, realizing this is probably more awkward for him than it is for you. Ask God frequently to temper your own reactions so that you don't disrupt your mate's exit from emotional seclusion.

Finally, don't compare your husband's or wife's extent of openness to that which you see in someone else. Focus on the amount of openness achieved and not the amount of disclosure that yet remains to be seen.

For You Who Are the Expressively Handicapped Mate

Take time alone to think out what you are feeling. Try to define it to your own satisfaction . . . as best as you can. You might even write out what you think you are feeling in an open letter to God. While doing so, ask him to make you increasingly comfortable in the presence of your own emotions and expressions.

Announce to your husband or wife that you want to begin talking more on a feeling level. Ask him at the same time to be patient with you and not to rush you along. Let him know you'll be clumsy at first, but assure him that if he will listen carefully—without reinterpreting everything—he will learn who you are.

Through reading and talking to others, search for the appropriate avenues to convey your emotions. Note how others do it—well-bodied, emotional people who are comfortable around their own innermost selves. You might even have lunch or breakfast with them and ask, "How did you learn to feel at ease talking about your own feelings?" You might even cite a specific circumstance you're facing and ask them, "What would you say if you were in my place?"

Stay on top of this area of growth. Though many of your efforts will be painful and uneasy, keep saying to yourself, "Talk." Ask God to free your lips so the words will flow more smoothly.

Don't give up . . . particularly in the early months. The long-term result is worth the upfront uneasiness. You'll be surprised at the new person you see emerging!

Reflection

Good emotional expression is a must for two-hearted intimacy. Therefore it is worth the time it takes to learn how to express and display your feelings before your mate.

Though it is true that men are often emotionally restricted or expressively bottled up, women can be as well. This is a problem experienced by both genders.

On the surface it might appear that a husband or wife is without emotion or feeling or interest, but usually underneath genuine soul movements are occurring which for one reason or another the unexpressive mate is unable to express.

A growing relationship takes into account the various styles of emotional expression each partner has and allows them both to exist without forcing either one to change.

Steps for Marital Growth

- ♥ As a man, can you describe some of the influences from your home and society that have encouraged you to mask or hold back your emotional expressions? What do you find hard about overcoming those past influences?

- ♥ As a woman, what parts of your emotional makeup do you wish your husband would develop? Which of those are uniquely feminine traits? Which ones do you think could become a part of your husband's character if he were willing to cultivate them?
- ♥ At an appropriate time, sit down together and discuss emotions. Agree to grow and preserve your relationship and encourage any needed change.

10

Honesty:

The Needed Alternative to Criticism

I wonder how many of you have found your experience to be like ours. There was a time in our marriage when Candee and I saw our conversations melting down like a hot nuclear reactor because what one of us was trying to convey, the other was mistaking for something entirely different. Understandably, there was a lot of unnecessary heat in our home that left the climate of our relationship unbalanced.

We've both possessed a driving hunger to do a flawless job of parenting. What parent hasn't? And because we wanted to be nearly perfect in our efforts with our kids, we've each worked relentlessly to find and use the right approaches to discipline and problem solving in order to cure those tough crises that faced both us and our toddlers and teenagers. Like you, we have often had varying opinions about which one was right. We have also discovered that the problems you have with your kids can quickly chill the joy in your romance.

While one of us was delivering a message to one of the

children or carrying out a correction, the other was watching with utter disbelief that anyone would handle a situation like that. When you least expect it, that old tendency surfaces again: My way is logical, yours is counterproductive.

What next? We began to hand out unsolicited judgments backed by good intentions. Many times we said things like:

> "If you really want this result, why didn't you say ____________________ to him instead of what you did?"

Or,

> "Why is it that you do ________________________ when you know that it's going to produce that effect?"

We've lost count of the times we have stood over each other while the other one was doing the best he knew how to correct some out-of-control situation. We've given each other advice while the wrong audience was listening. And we've found fault with the ways the other one was trying to work out his God-given responsibility of rearing and disciplining our children. Oh! That can be disasterous!

You know how it goes. You mean well. You know your motives are right. But what you utter inaugurates a disaster that may take from hours to days to overcome. It triggers a chilling effect in your relationship you know you can't afford.

Now, if you can't relate to that, how about this one? We used to try to help each other out by sharing some of the responsibilities around the home so we could have more time together later to enjoy some of life's quieter moments. When one would vacuum or dust, the other one would take issue with the order in which the tasks were carried out:

> "You know you don't do it like that. That just makes more work."

The big challenge was trying to find a hundred new ways of making the same appeal.

Then, when we moved from the interior work to the garage, the tension was even greater.

"When did you get the idea to wash the car in the sun where it would streak the paint? By the way, you left some smudges on the right rear window. You want to catch 'em? Let's get it right this time."

Paying Attention to Motives and Words

Peculiar, isn't it, how we can overlook both the motives and effort and become a judge of the quality of achievement? What happens? We feel we must be honest, so we point out each other's shortcomings and call attention to what could have been done as opposed to what was done. It's a matter of perspective. But so often when one of us feels we're being honest, the other hears it as criticism. That's the issue we have to deal with ourselves before our own hearts can slide in alongside the other and have the freedom to move through life situations together.

Frankly, Candee and I find in order to keep both our friendship and romance alive, we have to work at it continually. Subtle as it may seem to you, this is a serious problem area to most marriages. You can fly through the years together beleaguered by it unless you come to terms with the distinction between honesty and criticism. That's what we've done. And today, we work to say things that will avoid conveying wrong impressions.

We're not saying that we are overly sensitive, because we're not; or that we walk on eggs around each other, because we don't. But we have grown to care enough about each other's thoughts and feelings that we've found it worth the time and effort it takes to cultivate the communication of precise thoughts and encouraging suggestions. We put the pointed finger back in the holster and took up speaking with open hands and vulnerable, approachable hearts.

I think the following vignette from another couple's marriage will help to clarify the need to distinguish between honesty and criticism, which seem close to each other on the surface, but are worlds apart at the core.

When Jane walked into the office and sat down, it was apparent she was suffering. She'd driven several hours seeking counsel regarding her position in a marriage that was failing for the second time. She and her husband had divorced once before in their ten-year relationship. Jane had cried for days. This woman who was so attentive to her appearance remained behind sunglasses during the two-hour conversation. Across the spillway of hurt, bitterness, disappointment, and anger flowed her nervous—and stress-filled—words.

Unwrapping her thoughts, she described her husband in terms which left the impression that she had good reason for feeling despair. Here are three things she said of him that still stick in my mind:

> "He has no desire to grow. He seldom reads his Bible or anything else."
>
> "He has no love for our son. He rarely shows him any tenderness."
>
> "He has no interest in our relationship. He hardly spends time alone with me."

Before drawing any conclusions, we decided that Dave should be given the chance to come in. Jane warned that he wouldn't agree to such a suggestion. However, he did. Not only did he agree, he initiated the appointment. That was odd for a man who had "no desire . . . no love . . . no interest."

Two weeks later Dave came into the office. His interest and his wife's description didn't match. Jane's comments were introduced into our conversation while she sat next to him, and Dave was given the freedom to respond.

I have learned from counseling couples that most histories have two explanations, two viewpoints—and this one sure did. Here's what Dave said:

> I do study, and I do love God. But something has cooled my outward display of that. You see, Jane used to frequently ask me to read books or Scripture to her while she was cooking—books that were of interest to me. But she would spend the time *criticizing* the way I read and pronounced the words. Instead of keying in on the thoughts that were stimulating my growth, she focused on my inability to read and emphasize the

> terms her way. She prides herself in having more education than I, and I couldn't do or say anything right. So finally I said, "Why bother?" My interest hasn't changed, but my display has.
>
> About our son. I have withdrawn somewhat because being with him became awkward. Whenever I would spend time with him, Jane would stand over us and coach me in front of him: "Why do you handle him like that? Don't you think that you should . . . ?" The conclusions to the sentence vary. If I correct him, she criticizes me for being abusive and lacking in tenderness. But if she corrects him, she can raise her voice—even scream—and somehow her way is always acceptable.
>
> So far as our relationship is concerned, as often as we go out or away, she complains about the places I've chosen and the things I suggest; or she spends the time talking about how much she misses our boy. I've given up. It's not worth the constant strain. It always has to be her way. You lose long enough, and you withdraw in order to preserve what little harmony remains.

As we sat together and weighed Dave's responses against Jane's judgments, she said, "I'm not trying to tear you down, but if I don't tell you, who will?" There was the problem. She said she was speaking much-needed words of honest insight. He said she was exercising arbitrary, self-serving criticism. The two were miles apart.

What You Say or How You Say It

We often fail to make the distinction between honesty and criticism. It's not that our motives are necessarily wrong; it's those things that come naturally to us that produce a harmful effect. We don't hear the way our words come across to each other, and our tones and physical expressions betray us. What we say to someone else—our mates or our children—may sound like mere messages in our heads, yet in our hearer's minds the tones and expressions overshadow our best intentions. This is why I believe that it's not what you say that is most important, but how you say it that often plays the greater role.

Critical speech patterns often serve as substitutes for honesty. It is less painful that way. You see, not only does it hurt to be told the truth, it often hurts to tell the truth. Honesty requires conversation and dialogue, which in turn require work and sacrifice of one's own comfort.

Sometimes the difference between criticism and honesty is the difference between talking and telling, between interaction and sniping. Honesty requires openness and vulnerability. Criticism forces the other person to defend himself against our judgmental spirit when he has been predetermined to be wrong. Honesty, on the other hand, allows a person to explain himself so that if there's information that can change our wrong judgments, it can be freely given and objectively accepted.

There's yet another reason we engage in criticism and that is because we take it up as a habit. Sick as it may seem, some men and women find ill pleasure in tearing down their mates. I remember a neighbor who was caustic to her husband from the time she awoke to the moment she hit the sheets. The acid from her tongue was spilled all over everyone who came near her. The effect on the neighborhood was lethal. She'd even snap at the children who would ride their bikes on the public sidewalk in front of her home.

Criticism can become an unquenchable appetite, a way of life, and there can be just as vicious a battle to overcome it as to overcome greed, lust, anger, or controlled substances and chemicals. It's best to stop it in its earlier stages. Criticism kills.

I've learned that the majority of those addicted to criticism aren't necessarily unpleasant, unsocial people like our neighbor was. Instead, they've learned to mask the worst elements of their criticism with laughter and humor.

Floyd and Harriett Thatcher, in their book *Long-Term Marriage*, make the following observation:

> Very much like this dangerous and emotionally treacherous game of words is the poorly disguised "joking" put-down. It's amazingly easy to slide into

> this snide approach of venting dissatisfaction and hostility toward one's husband or wife: "Vera's still got a good figure. There's just more of it than there used to be, but most of it is still in the right places." But the words and tone of voice underline the fact that Vera's weight is a bone of contention in their home—and probably not the only one at that.
>
> The jesting (critical) remark, loaded with innuendo, is without doubt one of the cruelest and most devastating and unfunny bits of verbal disaster to rock any marriage. It may start off in low key, as did a former friend's joking comments about his wife's superabundant breast measurements. But this attitude only inched slowly but surely to a habit of snide put-downs to cover his own inadequacy until their marriage was wrecked and debris spoiled at least two lives![1]

If you want a union where two living souls are honored and preserved because they have God-breathed worth, then you must decide that criticism—humorous or otherwise, well-intended or cruel—has no place in your life. Get rid of it. Doing so will charge the atmosphere of your cheapened relationship with respect and perhaps a newfound sense of security.

One wife, Pam, whom I interviewed recently, said:

> For twenty-five years I've been the target of Hugh's sick humor, laden with criticism, and I've finally had enough. I've tolerated it publicly for all those years, but no more. While everyone else has been laughing, I've been dying . . . my love's been dying as well.

Is your mate thinking similar thoughts? It could be that he is and you don't know it. Those of us who are prone to be "Hughs" in life are oblivious to the pain we're causing our "Pams." If we are, then we must ask ourselves, "Will I push him (or her) to the point of no return, as Hugh did Pam? Or will I take the initiative to stop, seek forgiveness, and salvage that which is

---

1. Floyd and Harriet Thatcher, *Long-Term Marriage* (Waco, Tex.: Word Books, Inc., 1980), p. 81.

more priceless to me than what I've been admitting by my behavior?"

Is It Honesty or Criticism?

We need to get honesty and criticism clearly defined in our minds before we can accurately evaluate our own patterns, checking to see just where we are, and then determining the direction we need to move.

Honesty is the state or act of speaking truthful thoughts and feelings in straightforward fashion, using the approaches with one another that show fairness and respect. Being honest requires frankness or candor that is clothed with both sensitivity and pure motives.

By contrast, *criticism* is the action of making judgments, finding fault, censuring, and showing disapproval because others don't do or say things the way we prefer. And though there are no clear-cut rights or wrongs involved, criticism prompts us to make it sound like our ways are God's ways, and we defend them as such.

In taking inventory of our own experiences these past two decades, Candee and I have come to the following conclusions about honesty when compared to criticism. The reason we know so much about them is that we've observed them firsthand in our own relationship. And we might add that these conclusions help us today to know what we want and why it is worth the effort to get it and preserve it. In reviewing them, see if you feel the same way. We hope both of you will agree with us. If not, then perhaps one of you is suffering in your relationship because criticism has gained the favored position in the daily affairs of your home.

Here are the comparisons:

- Honesty often hurts; criticism always inflicts injury.
- Honesty promotes healing; criticism promotes pain.
- Honesty speaks with an open hand; criticism speaks with a pointed, alienating finger.

- Honesty has no games; criticism plays games that are endless in variety.
- Honesty wishes the ultimate good for both; criticism seeks only the good of its source.
- Honesty makes facts and principles its business; criticism feeds on assumptions and unrealistic expectations.
- Honesty is unselfish; criticism wants only its own way.
- With honesty, both win. With criticism, both unquestionably lose.

As Candee and I caught on to this battle of honesty and criticism in our own marriage and friendship, we began identifying the phrases we were using to introduce our criticisms to each other. Once you can stand outside yourself and grab an objective glimpse, then you can go back in, and with the Lord's help activate new patterns for growth. Today, when we see those phrases leak from our lips like a toxic spill, we stop immediately and choose a more honest path of monologue or dialogue—whichever is most appropriate.

Here are some of those phrases we were using to introduce our criticisms:

"Why is it that you always (or never) . . . ?"

"When are you going to start . . . ?"

"Why do I always have to be the one who . . . ?"

"Can't you ever do it right?"

"Anyone can see that . . . !"

"If you truly cared, you would. . . ."

Abrasive lines, aren't they? In fact, when you are on the receiving end of them, you find yourself becoming defensive and sometimes hostile. Right? Sure you do.

When you are accustomed to dispensing such statements, you don't hear them for what they really are. You're deaf to the way they come across to the hearer. But when you are on the receiving end, it takes all you have to keep your mouth shut. And sometimes we can't do that too well, and then all hell breaks loose.

Most of us can relate to the situation David Augsburger describes in his book *Caring Enough to Confront.* Change a few of the details and the scene has taken place in your home, just as it has in ours. Here is how he tells it:

> It's the end of a usual evening. You're stretched out in your favorite chair, when your wife pulls up beside you, pad and pencil in hand.
>
> "May I read you the collected sayings of Chairman You- know-who from the moment you got home until now?"
>
> "Yeah, if it's all that good," you say.
>
> "Okay, 5:35, 'Hi, I'm home.' 6:20, 'Hamburger again? That all we can afford?' 7:14, 'How come the paper's wet?' 8:03, 'Switch the channel. That's a lousy show.'"
>
> "Look," you say, "you wanted talk? Why didn't you marry [Donahue]?"
>
> "All I want is a little companionship," she says. "You walk in the door, say 'Hi,' then take a vow of silence."
>
> "No, you missed something," you reply. "I walk in, say 'Hi.' You give me that I'm-burned-up-that-you're-late-again look and I know that silence is my only safety, so I shut up. That's why I withdraw."
>
> "You've got it just backwards," she responds. "You withdraw, and the only way I can get any response out of you is to do a little prodding."
>
> That's when it hits you. The two of you are saying the same thing. But each is saying the other starts it. Maybe it's one continuous cycle. I nag, you withdraw, I nag, you withdraw, I nag, you withdraw.
>
> "Honey," you say, "who cares which came first—your prodding or my silence. We're stuck in this cycle. How can we break it?"

"I guess I could say something warm instead of digging at you."

"Okay, and I'll say what I really want instead of withdrawing."[2]

Changing the Pattern

The question is, how do you get over the hump and through the barriers so that criticism, blame, judging, and so on no longer hold you back and away from each other? The answer is as simple as five words: *Speak the truth in love!* Ah! Learning to do that perhaps is the same as deciding to do it.

Lots of situations are like that. For example, dieting or exercise. You can search indefinitely to find a plan or program that gives you results with the least amount of effort. Some search, never to find, while others simply decide to start something—anything—and without making a federal case of it, they win! Why? Because they did immediately what had to be done with or without a plan. They said, "I am going to do it regardless of the pain, and I am starting at this moment." In so many cases, good plans naturally emerge from the determination to change. Whether a plan is crude or polished, simple or sophisticated, it often makes little difference. In the end, it's not the plan that is important, it is the result.

Start now, wherever it makes the most sense to you to start. Decide to speak truth in love and get going with the project. Use any way of getting there that makes immediate sense to you. God will take care of the rest.

Regarding the background to this counsel, Paul has written a letter to his Christian friends in Ephesus about the ministry of the church and the way the body of Christ was to develop and grow into a strong, healthy organism. In Ephesians 4:15-16 he links truth-speaking in love with growth and shows how it fits in a contrast between childlike and adultlike behaviors.

On this point, a marriage is no different from a ministry.

2. David Augsburger, *Caring Enough to Confront* (Glendale, Calif.: Regal Books, 1978), pp. 10-11.

So think of marriage—your marriage—as you read these words that are wrapped around Paul's encouragement to "speak the truth in love." He tells us:

> We are no longer to be children, tossed here and there by waves, and carried about by every wind of doctrine, by the trickery of men, by craftiness in deceitful scheming; but speaking the truth in love, we are to grow up in all aspects into Him, who is the head, even Christ."

You see it? Speaking the truth in love by practice paves the way for growth in all aspects. Your marriage, my marriage, is no exception. Yet it's right there that most of us struggle. Either we speak truth without love or we speak what we think to be kind words without complete truth. Both ways we can lose—and often do! Again, in many of our relationships the stranger—the outsider—often gets the kinder treatment. Thus we bury the very marriages we hope to resurrect. A mature union sees honesty as an operational norm, not an exception; and certainly not something you do only on Sundays as a response to the religious service.

Now would be an appropriate time for many of you to reenter the realm of 1 Corinthians 13 and run a check on your speaking and response patterns with each other. If you can speak true words without letting your verbal foot step over the boundaries set down by the apostle Paul, then you're on your way to maturity. And criticism will be put behind you, and one more barrier to beautiful, free-spirited growth will be removed from your friendship and romance.

Getting from One Scene to the Other

Okay, let's put all this together by underscoring this statement. *Only truth spoken in love will draw together and set the stage for further growth.*

If you are looking for some helpful ideas on how to get the job done and cover this base, then I believe the following will help you.

First, *choose to be aggressively honest* with each other. If you have decided to do so, be sure to inform your husband or wife that you've made this commitment so he is not overcome and paralyzed by sudden surprise. Acknowledge that you might be clumsy at first, but that you are trying to do what's best for both of you, awkward as it may be in the beginning. Tell him you invite his feedback if your attempts seem abrasive or self-righteous. Keep in mind that not only is honesty essential, but so is the dressing you give to it. Take time to learn how to do it right.

Next, *screen your comments carefully*. Think before unloading. If you're uncertain how to screen your speech, then accept these five guidelines as safeguards for your intentions.

- *Be clear.* Take care to see that the other person understands you, and be slow in getting upset if it is taking him longer to receive your message than you think it should take.
- *Be up-front.* Don't couch your statements in humor. Save the funny stuff for the good times when you both feel settled. Never take the "back door" approach to problem solving. Say what's on your mind and run it through the filters of gentleness and tenderness. If these don't come naturally to you, then you're going to have to cultivate those filters in your heart.
- *Be brief.* Work to develop the skill of saying what's on your heart without saying something more, something less, or something else. Incidentally, if your mate violates one of these five, be tolerant. It takes a lifetime to get it all together.
- *Pay close attention to timing.* Constructive information often loses its impact because it was dumped on its hearer when the hearer was on overload or perhaps preoccupied by some other crisis or catastrophe. If you have something important to say, then don't ruin it by communicating it prematurely just to get it off your own chest.
- *Get accustomed to asking yourself good questions beforehand.* For example: Who is going to benefit by

what I am about to say? Me? Them? *Us* together? If the answer isn't one of the last two, then put your words on hold until you can get your motives right.

When you cultivate your relationship in the garden bed of criticism, the best you can expect is crop failure. However, when you cultivate it in the soil of honesty and loving speech, you can expect full and triumphant growth.

Reflection

Couples who want heartfelt communication must be willing to speak the truth to one another—learning how to distinguish between honesty and criticism.

Often the difference lies not in what is said, but in the manner or spirit in which it is communicated.

Caring mates take time and effort to cultivate the expression of precise thoughts and encouraging suggestions. They learn how to speak openly, with vulnerable, approachable hearts.

Cultivation of expression means that we must work to hear the way we send our messages . . . to try to read them as our mate does.

The art of talking with an open and nonthreatening heart is developed over a long period of time, but is well worth the pain and effort once it comes into full bloom.

Only truth spoken in love will draw mates together and set the stage for further growth.

Steps for Marital Growth

♥ Remember, the apostle Paul spoke of one's speaking truth in love as being a sign of his or her maturity. According to his thought, honesty alone wasn't to be held up as a priority, but saying things with honesty bathed in love—that was to be the objective. Take time to make some distinctions between those two things. In your own terms, what is involved in wrapping love around truthful communication?

- ♥ We also made the statement that "Sometimes the difference between criticism and honesty is the difference between talking and telling, between interaction and sniping." Further develop those thoughts.

11

Renewal:

The Priority of Decisive Partners

Few marriages of today's times are adequately prepared to survive the prolonged strains they live under, particularly those strains produced by jobs, parenting, aging, and sickness. The shell of the union may last, but the spirit of the marriage will more than likely wither and disintegrate unless mates get periodic reprieves from the pressure. In time strain and pressure distort. They turn fresh love into spoilage. They cause husbands and wives to grow blind to their original commitments and decided priorities. Time and again strain and pressure silence laughter, provoking restlessness and tension. Add to that—*distance.*

Regardless of how strong individuals or marriages seem to be, the weight of stress can squash down and thin out those strengths. It accentuates the cracks in a person's character which are otherwise not seen.

Besides work, normal parenting demands, and the inevitable effects of growing old, there are other things beyond our control which can place strain on a romance: a terminally ill child, a dependent and dying parent, a financial reverse, a wayward son or daughter, a hateful neighbor, or tension in one's extended family. Undoubtedly you can add to this list things that have put strain on top of your own union.

Regardless of the source of pressure or the mix of stresses, couples need to escape them long enough to catch a breath or to recapture their souls; long enough to get reacquainted or to realign their purposes; to be refreshed or to regain a comfort level once shared in trust.

Some time around the beginning of the seventeenth century, Miguel de Cervantes wrote:

> The bow cannot always stand bent, nor can human frailty subsist without some lawful recreation.

What he noticed about human capacity in his own times is just as true for modern men and women, and more specifically, married couples. The bow of their marriage cannot stand constant tension or stress triggered by outside sources. In time, the partners will snap or shatter. And that's precisely what has happened to couples surrounding us. They allowed their union to be sucked dry by prevailing strains which themselves could have been better managed by some well-taken, well-planned quiet hours spent together.

It's possible that at this moment you may be thinned out under the strain of things. You haven't taken a break from the situation you're in, and the end still isn't in sight. If so, I encourage you to find a way of momentary escape where the two of you can catch your breath and allow your hearts to get back on line with one another.

The Need for Childless Moments

In our own marriage, Candee and I have found that the key to keeping our cherished friendship alive has been breaking away long enough to keep ourselves fresh and our love growing. We've found that keeping *us* alive is almost the same as keeping our marriage healthy and vigorous.

We have discovered that partners can't rely on family vacations alone to provide them this much needed space for renewal.

However, we have learned from our own experience that family furloughs—fun as they may be—seem to favor family development rather than couple growth.

Our four are special to us, just as yours are to you. We not only love them, we like them. Unquestionably! They add such a repertoire of treasures to our lives. But the truth is, when they are present our attention is divided and our conversations are fragmented. You can hardly say a complete paragraph—perhaps even a sentence—without having your thoughts tripped and your words interrupted.

Thus we concluded long ago that we need alternative times alone, times when we can have our world around us quiet and calm so that we can contend with each other without distraction. Sometimes those occasions are an hour or so, sometimes they're ours for a few days. Whichever, with each other the purpose is the same: *relinking our hearts and heads.*

We now do this regularly. We couldn't survive otherwise. But it never ceases to amaze us that couples go for years before finally seizing some quiet, tranquil hours as a pair. At least a dozen times lately we have been surprised by friends married a minimum of ten years who have just now begun taking steps toward their first "childless weekends."

The Lost Art of Togetherness

Now, not all folks postpone being alone because of family needs. Some avoid such undistracted moments simply because they have lost the art of being together. They have lost the ability to talk face to face for extended periods of time. They have become strangers with the same name who now fear being left by themselves in the same car or in a shared remote hotel room or condominium because they'd have to admit to their acquired distance and lost sense of touch.

Couples who have drifted from each other tend to be tense when they find themselves with no one else around. They walk on eggs in order to avoid the vast number of sensitive issues bearing *off limits* signs. They're ill-prepared for the tough but necessary discussions. And besides, they find it far more difficult to get reacquainted a second, third, or fourth time than it was in the first round of their courtship and early marriage.

Candee and I have known the feeling ourselves. We survived one stretch of demands some time ago that kept our attention riveted to focal points outside our relationship. Finally we took the opportunity to break away from our pressures (maybe *distractions* is a better term) that had shoved us into opposite corners.

For both of us, the thought of getting away for ten days all by ourselves was exhilarating. But for me the exhilaration was slightly blunted by the reality that we were going to have to do something we hadn't done for a while: *talk*. Just to each other. Alone! One on one. No competition. Any subjects we wanted.

"Could we do that? What will we talk about? Will we talk ourselves out before we get there? How will we approach our neglected conversations that will finally come due?" These were the questions that poked holes in my confidence. Thus we headed off on our holiday wondering whether our time alone would result in disaster or delight.

Not only was my worst fear quickly resolved, but ten days passed and we had some subjects left over. Once we started and got beyond those introductory cautions, both our tongues loosened while our hearts renewed their responses to one another.

We've seen couples with similar questions fail—even if only one possessed them. Believing the worst, they allowed little excuses to defer their holidays, and they continued their unbroken routine of responsibility. How tragic!

Seeking the Quiet Hour

Couples who are concerned about their marriages must come to the point of saying "no" to the strains and demands on their lives. There isn't any alternative. No, you won't consume our union; No, you won't rip from us the satisfaction a healthy marriage can provide; No, you won't steal from us any longer the soul we once shared.

The best way to say no is not by making tentative plans for getting alone. Saying no occurs when a husband and wife—scared as they may be—finally walk away from their strains and pressures long enough to regroup and regrow. Take it by faith. Strains and pressures will survive apart from your being there. They need no help to exist. But your marriage won't. Neglect it long enough, serve everything and everyone else instead, and eventually it will succumb.

Quiet hours are those that are free of the familiar, that are experienced away from the immediate routine. Quiet hours are hours when the noise and complaints of kids, clients, pupils, parishioners, patients, and colleagues are no longer heard. Quiet hours are those during which you have no obligation to be somewhere on time, which do not obligate you to wake up with the ring of the alarm. Quiet hours are those which don't have a time limit on them.

Quiet hours allow souls to lie back, to listen to God, to hear the speech patterns of caring mates, and to respond accordingly. A quiet hour allows one to lay down and pick up a conversation several times during its course.

Quiet Hours of Varied Sorts

Candee and I find our quiet hours, our hours for renewal, have been of two sorts: abbreviated and prolonged. An abbreviated quiet hour may seem to contradict what we've just said. But it doesn't, perhaps because of the frame of mind we have developed.

Our *abbreviated* quiet hours are those we enjoy either in the mid-morning, mid-afternoon, early evening, or during a day off. It's during these one-, two-, or three-hour blocks that we grab moments over coffee or over a simple and inexpensive meal. For us, some of the best settings for soul-linking have been in unnoticed corners of coffee shops and restaurants during off hours. Coffee, tea, split meals, desserts—those have been our passports to such plentiful hideaways. But in each case the eating has been secondary to the actual opportunity of just being together . . . traveling through each other's thoughts and feelings. We often enter as two and leave as one.

We've always loved the sea. We can walk or sit together, feeling the breeze, inhaling the salt air, or maybe wade along the water's edge. Times like these season a good conversation just as sage, rosemary, and thyme add life to an otherwise ordinary meal.

But whatever it is that makes a setting conducive to a quiet hour for you, it's important to hand select it. When Candee and I seize our special moments, we want the setting to help support the happenings of our heart. For that reason, the two of us stay away from malls and shopping outlets, with their host of manufactured goods that can lure our attention away from each other. Urges to acquire only create competition our hungry souls don't need. Instead, we search for environments that will allow us to sit next to each other, to have eye contact; settings where we won't easily be distracted, where we will be inclined to talk, and to talk privately. If there is a need to argue, we want to do it where the ears of the community can't hear. And if we want to speak tenderly, we want to be where we can do so without an audience.

On the other hand, our prolonged hours are times we can rob our schedules of a few days. Our abbreviated moments tide us over until these "main events!" In fact, we can tolerate all kinds of pressure if we know one of these extended spells is waiting up the road for us.

For our extended times of soul-to-soul retreat, we have watched ourselves of late returning to the same two spots. Why? Because we escape a lot of the strain and adjustment of breaking away by going back to familiar places where we know we'll feel comfortable and where we have made prior heart-bonding memories.

Each time that you try a new place or a new area, you burn up a lot of emotional energy as you negotiate between yourselves. "Is this place clean enough for you? Do you feel comfortable with the decor and surroundings? This restaurant look okay? Or would you like to try someplace else?" If you are like us, your budget has dictated that you get the nicest places for the most reasonable prices. And in the search process, you have had disasters, as we've had. We have come to realize that when we are alone we want the fewest hindrances to affect our times. Returning to a handful of favorite spots eliminates the risk.

The joy of our extended quiet times was also enhanced when we caught on to the pattern that characterized our earlier times together. In fact, things that used to sidetrack our enjoyment no longer do because we're prepared for them.

Specifically, the weekends would cycle through three stages: *conflict, adjustment* and *comfort*. When we caught on to this pattern, we'd mention it to others and invariably they'd smile, look at one another, and say, "Funny thing, that perfectly describes our times alone, too."

You know, sometimes just knowing that you are not alone in a particular problem gives you the broader perspective you need to crawl up above the struggle. If the pattern—as we sketch it for you—describes your situation, then perhaps you can develop a strategy to win over it as we have. We refuse to get caught in its jaws . . . especially the first stage of the cycle: conflict.

Inevitably when Candee and I get the opportunity to leave town for a few days, the moment is long overdue. The pattern used to be that one of us finally got the opportunity to have silence or to lie back, rest, and watch some TV. The other had finally gained the occasion to talk without interference, to go outside and get active, to do a little reading and planning for the future.

There's nothing wrong with these activities, but they can collide if the prime reason for going away is to be together. In the first hour of the motor trip the storm of emotions would let loose and then it seemed to take almost twelve hours—overnight— for the cloud to break up.

What was the reason for the conflict? Always it was rigid expectations for what the finally arrived moment should be. That was stage one!

Stage two was adjustment. Both of us would mellow overnight, realizing that that was no way to spend a preciously short time. So before breakfast we would make a negotiated settlement that embodied somehow the strongest of both our desires. Then we proceeded through the next twenty-four to thirty-six hours working at that plan with an agreement to be flexible.

Stage three was comfort. In this part of the cycle we lived with the peaceful benefits sticking with the plan brought us—a little eating, some walking, a bit of riding along the bayside, an agreed upon movie.

Because we are now aware of these stages of the cycle, we can work to circumvent stage one, and before we leave home we work on the stage two. We negotiate things ahead of time to synchronize our expectations.

I hope mentioning this will help you salvage many more of your quiet hours together, be they abbreviated or prolonged.

Priority of the Quiet Hour Honored in Scripture

For those of you who seek biblical precedents for the things you do in your individual and married lives, I can think of at least three occasions from Scripture in which we see quietness or solitude upheld as a priority. Each is quite different. And incidentally, these not only apply to a needed individual discipline in our lives, but fit with the disciplines mates should share together as one.

The first involved the prophet Elijah. He was overcome by fear. He'd lost perspective. A look at the text reveals that he had extended himself well beyond his emotional strength, and he succumbed to stiff depression. Instinctively he went off to find a solitary place to run from his pressures. He parked himself under a juniper tree and slept. Twice an angel of the Lord awakened him and fed him, and the energy and strength he gained from that setting enabled him to travel on to Mt. Horeb. In his quiet hour Elijah became physically and emotionally recharged.

Christ himself sought hours of quietness. Not only those where away from the masses he sought the face of God the Father, but he also made his way to Bethany to be with some friends he cherished. Apparently, in his humanity he wearied as we do. So for the sake of renewal he traveled south to a favored hideaway, a home with those he loved. Somehow they added encouragement to him.

Another example of the need for a quiet hour is found in Psalm 46, a piece composed by an obscure group of brothers known to their times as the sons of Korah. These men from a levitical family shared in the music ministry of the Temple. The song in general describes a dimension of God he's chosen to show to man in so many ways. The lyrics tell us:

> God is our refuge and strength,
> A very present [on time, never late]
> help in trouble
> (Psalm 46:1).

Next the lyricists describe a context of trouble that includes natural catastrophes and international tensions, and then God's relationship to them.

After telling of God's supportive involvements in the lives of his people, the brothers quote God's own words revealed to them which extend themselves into the whole spectrum of life:

> "Cease striving and know that I am God" (Psalm 46:10).

The King James translators render the phrase,

> "Be still and know that I am God."

The editors of the NASB add the word *striving* for clarity. But the action God calls for is ceasing, being still. In the Hebrew the term means to sink down, to let drop.

As one looks at the psalm, he soon realizes there is a connection between stillness, dropping back, sinking down—so as to reflect and evaluate—and knowing. Man cannot know God intimately apart from moments of stillness and breaking with the routine.

And the point I want to underscore with you is that what is true for us in the vertical realm is true also in the horizontal realm. Knowing one another, being of one heart and mind, cannot occur apart from finding the equivalence of stillness and ceasing in our marital unions. That equivalence I am calling the quiet hours. And it is in the realm of these moments that the priority of renewal is honored by decisive mates.

In a practical sense, how is this stillness exercised? It is exercised through three concerns:

First, it means finding the appropriate setting where a still moment can be best captured and shared.

Second, it means refining a plan to counteract the distractions that can lead to conflict.

And third, it means sinking down and dropping back emotionally, and fine-tuning the senses to see and hear what's truly going on in each other's inner spaces.

What Couples Need, Individuals Need As Well

Not only do we need to have quiet hours that we can share together as married partners, but we individually need moments of calm and solitude when we can corral our thoughts and emotions. I have found that if I can collect my own loose ends, then I am able to bring a quieter spirit into our relationship. And Candee and I have found that that is important for both of us to do. Calmer individuals build calmer unions.

The author my wife and I cherish the most is Anne Morrow Lindbergh and her work *Gift from the Sea*. In her recollections, she records the thinking of a woman who took time annually to be still. In doing so she got to know herself and her God better. Amid the demands of the life she and her reknowned husband Charles shared, she found a crack to periodically crawl out through in order to find relief. To us the beauty of Charles's and Anne's relationship is that he allowed her the freedom to break away. Each time she returned from her quiet hour with a more durable strength with which to meet the needs of her family—including her husband.

In her third chapter, entitled "Moon Shell," she inscribes these words:

> Women need solitude in order to find again the true essence of themselves: that firm strand which will be the indispensable center of a whole web of human re-

> lationships. She must find that inner stillness which Charles Morgan describes as "the stilling of the soul within the activities of the mind and body so that it might be still as the axis of a revolving wheel is still."[1]

She continues:

> This beautiful image is to my mind the one that women could hold before their eyes. This is an end toward which we could strive—to be the still axis within the revolving wheel of relationships, obligations, and activities. Solitude alone is not the answer to this; it is only a step toward it, a mechanical aid, like the "room of one's own" demanded for women, before they could make their place in the world. The problem is not entirely in finding the room of one's own, the time alone, difficult and necessary as this is. The problem is more how to still the soul in the midst of its activities. In fact, the problem is how to feed the soul.[2]

Within her piece she clarifies also that what is needed for women is needed also for their male counterparts. And I would add that it is needed for a marriage as well.

Recently, Candee was overspent. And though we both needed a shared reprieve, she needed the break a bit more at that moment. Having learned the value of stilling the soul and thus experiencing renewal, we agreed the priority was to let the most needy one find a quiet moment beyond our county limits. We shifted responsibilities that weekend and made the necessary adjustments to our schedule. Though it was Candee who slipped gently away from home, both of us benefited.

She so appreciated the quiet hour that she penned the following words onto a card and gave it to me as she entered the door of our home:

---

1. Anne Morrow Lindbergh, *Gift from the Sea* (New York: Pantheon Books, 1955, 1975), pp. 50-51.

2. Ibid., p. 51.

Sweetheart,

Sometimes just being close is enough. And sometimes having a little space is even better. Thank you for giving me the opportunity to leave. I needed the time alone. I love you and am looking forward to our times together in many new settings.

With deep and committed love,

One couple I know has discovered this to be healthy for their relationship also. Their love is deep. Their marriage is solid. But they need moments alone, too—not because their bond is impaired or troubled, but because they come back to each other stronger individuals who feel more rested. And both are well aware of the benefits they enjoy as a result of this arrangement.

Margaret takes her leaves locally each spring. She feels more comfortable with that. In the fall, Bob goes off to a monastery in a distant state to join other laymen, along with a handful of monks, taking a quiet break from the revolving world. The impact on their marriage has been so noticeable that today Margaret won't even allow Bob to consider not going. She makes sure he gets there.

A Word to the Fearful

I realize that the thought of being alone together conjures up concerns of the worst kind for some of you. You're sure you can't pull it off, based upon your history. Yet you not only realize it is important, but down deep would really like to do so.

Where do you begin? How do you make it work?

Well, I suggest you begin with abbreviated quiet hours, the sort where you start with small increments of time: an hour here, a few hours there. The idea is to work up to a weekend somewhere off in the future. You need not rush it. In time you will get there, really. But build up to it. That's what is important.

It's for You to Decide

Do you grab moments alone? Do you make renewal and the seizing of quiet hours a high priority of your relationship? If not,

I appeal to you to begin. Soon! The demands will always be there. Demands seem to be waiting in line seeking your attention. They have a conspiracy to keep you enslaved.

I can't take your quiet hours for you any more than you can take mine for me. But if you want a marriage and friendship that's growing in its most intimate dimensions, you won't be able to attain that desire until you enjoy both abbreviated and prolonged soul-moments with each other in still and undistracted settings.

I hope I've stimulated your appetite for some time alone. How about beginning at once to plan some soul-moments together where renewal can come as a result of the time you spend away from it all?

Reflection

Although the shell of a union may endure, the spirit of the marriage may disintegrate in time unless mates take periodic and shared reprieves from the pressures they live under.

The pressures we must often escape are not those we create for ourselves, but those brought into our lives from the outside. Nonetheless they can wear our relationships thin.

The key to keeping a cherished friendship alive may be found in breaking away long enough and frequently enough to keep ourselves fresh and our love growing. And usually that involves childless weekends.

Without such moments of focused attention, it's difficult to keep the kind of updated knowledge of one another that keeps two hearts in close proximity alive and growing together.

Not only do couples need shared moments of solitude and renewal, but on occasion individual mates may need to be alone in order to revitalize themselves and stay on top of their own development.

A growing marriage needs refreshed inhabitants!

Steps for Marital Growth

- Identify the most intense form of pressure affecting your marriage. Does the pressure affect you both equally, or do you sense it more than does your mate?
- Discuss with your mate the times you've shared alone that have had the most healthy impact on your marriage. What did you do on those occasions that caused you to draw together? What things did you do that you now favor the most . . . things you'd like to do again given the time and resources?
- If you feel uncomfortable being alone with your mate, spend some time defining the reasons. At an appropriate time, share with him in order to discover ways of reducing the tension and increasing your comfort level.
- How soon will it be before you take another shared reprieve together? Go get your calendar and block off a weekend before the thought wears off!

12

Memories:

The Wealth of Growing Soul Mates

If I had the power to unlock your mind, what would I find pressed between its pages? Pleasant, attractive, vibrant memories? Or ones that are predominantly bitter and abrasive? Are you trying to choke down the things of the past, or are you resting peaceably in the warm remembrances you've taken the time to create?

Think a minute and ask yourself this question: In the last year, how many affirming memories have my mate and I carved out together and stored in our chest of mental treasures? . . . memories for ourselves and for our children.

The Early Roots of Remembering

The work of building and recalling memories has its roots in the Old Testament. Apparently God saw the deep-seated need for his folks to experience occasions where accompanying joy and pleasure, pain and victory would later yield life-giving energy. If he viewed it to be important for them, then we need to take his concern seriously—particularly for our homes and our marriages. We need to fashion good memories for ourselves now which we can rummage through and dress ourselves in the future.

One of the earliest instances of memory-building surfaces in a rather sober happening in the life of the ancient Jews. The time was just prior to the actual passover and subsequent exodus from Egypt. From the period of Jacob and his sons' migration to Egypt until the time of Moses, the Jews' mobility had been cut to servitude of the worst sort. Desperately they cried to God for relief, and he listened to them. He raised up a deliverer for them who had the awkward job of trying to negotiate the Jews' release with a notorious pharaoh. Along with his dealings, God brought nine severe plagues that touched everyone's lives and toughened the tyrant's heart.

In those final hours of bondage, God gave Moses and Aaron instructions that would equip his chosen folk to survive the tenth and final plague—death—and make possible their long-awaited escape. The plan for protection is unveiled for us in Exodus 12:1-14, but I want to call your attention to the last three verses of this text:

> For I will go through the land of Egypt on that night, and will strike down all the first-born in the land of Egypt, both man and beast; and against all the gods of Egypt I will execute judgments—I am the LORD. And the blood shall be a sign for you on the houses where you live; and when I see the blood I will pass over you, and no plague will befall you to destroy you when I strike the land of Egypt. Now this day will be a *memorial* [a memory] to you, and you shall celebrate it as a feast to the LORD; throughout your generations you are to celebrate it as a permanent ordinance (emphasis added).

Within that broader text there are several things worth noting:

> These are words the Lord issued directly to Moses and Aaron (v. 1).

> This command inaugurated a new Jewish calendar (v. 2).
>
> These instructions were intended for the entire congregation of Israel (v. 3).

And a *sacred memory* was in the making: "This day will be a memorial to you . . . throughout your generations you are to celebrate it . . ." (v. 14).

Understanding a couple of terms draws our attention into the flow of this passage. The word *celebrate* has the thought of "making a pilgrimage." Its basic idea is to keep a feast or to observe a holiday; and in this instance there is a celebration of God's act of sparing the Israelites while all the first-born of Egypt died.

The term *memorial* stems from the word meaning "to think about, to recite or proclaim." God was about to do something supernatural for the Jews, and in the future he wanted their minds to come back to a remembrance of the love and goodness he had showed them.

Forty years later when the second generation of refugees were finally about to enter into the land reserved for them, Moses picked up on the same theme as he issued his final instructions to the people just prior to his death:

> "You shall *remember* all the way which the LORD your God has led you in the wilderness . . ." (Deuteronomy 8:2, emphasis added).

You see, the wilderness had great significance to the wanderers, as did the Passover. Why? Because God used it to humble them (v. 2), to test them in order to know what was in their hearts (v. 2), to teach them that man only lives by the words that proceed from his mouth (v. 3), and to do good for them in the end (v. 16). All of those objectives added up to a concern on God's part to mature the people he loved dearly.

In this instance, the primary reason for playing back the memories was so the Jews could call to mind the times God had walked with them, before them, and behind them.

> Their memories were . . . to keep their minds riveted to the reality that God alone was to be their life and solitary focus for living.
>
> . . . to keep them on target, constantly holding before them God's will for their lives.
>
> . . . to encourage humility, reminding them that God was the sole reason for their physical and spiritual survival.

There are other instances in the Bible of times memories or memorials played a significant role in people's experience. For example, the times related to the memorial stones from the Jordan River (Joshua 4:1-8), and to the Ebenezer stone associated with Samuel (1 Samuel 7). The stones taken from the Jordan were significant because they represented the moment God stepped in to shut off the flow of water for their convenient and safe passage across the river. The Ebenezer stone which Samuel set up between Mizpah and Shen represented to the people whom God had protected that "thus far the Lord has helped us."

Many of us have our own ebenezers. In fact, some have entire museums of them in their homes. We have our own collection which includes a large fragment of wood that exploded from a tree hit by lightening.

Several years back, Candee and several teenage students were hiking a rain-drenched trail in Yosemite, looking for shelter. Suddenly, a streak of electricity bolted to the ground, sending current through a tree and into the wet soil surrounding it. Several of the kids were stunned and bruised by the blast. Realizing that God had preserved her life and the lives of the teenagers, Candee grabbed a piece of tree bark and carried it with her as she and the others continued their escape from the thunder-throbbing wilderness. Why? Because she wanted a permanent remembrance—an ebenezer to remind our family that thus far the Lord had helped us again!

Periodically we drag out that old piece of bark to reexperience the impact of that moment in our lives. It has been a faith-builder for us, and especially for our dear children, who find its message unmistakably clear.

Bitter Experiences Turned Sweet

Thomas Fuller, the seventeenth-century clergyman from England, said, "That which is bitter to endure may be sweet to remember." We have certainly found this to be true.

Lafayette, Indiana. Early in our marriage, Candee and I moved to northern Indiana to spend time with students at Purdue University. Since both of us had grown up in sun-drenched southern California, we weren't prepared for what moved in on us about mid-November or early December. The winter was bitter. Cold winds swept down from the Great Lakes to refrigerate everything.

On short notice, we were forced to learn how to drive across icy bridges and cope with frozen plumbing for days on end. What was difficult became disastrous when we learned that we were going to be parents.

We lived in a large house located on the main highway two miles north of town. The place had been divided up into four apartments. Each of the other apartments was occupied by male students who knew nothing about cooking except how to disguise bad taste with excessive spices. Dinnertime was distressing to Candee, who was afflicted with "round-the-clock" sickness, because we lived in that quarter of the home where all the vents intersected. Each evening as the students returned home for dinner, she'd migrate to the corner of a remote closet with a bottle of Vicks to disguise the smell.

Our biggest headache was the plumbing. It froze repeatedly, causing us to make mega-trips two miles south to the nearest Shell station. We must have driven a couple extra thousand miles that winter to remain comfortable.

What a tough experience it was at the time. We didn't laugh much then. But today it is a sweet remembrance for us. We clutched each other through that second winter of our marriage.

Thank God things thaw!

Grad school . . . fifth year. Carrying the weight of four

children, each other, multiple jobs, and studying, we found ourselves numerous times on our knees staring at sanity's edge. On occasion, we wondered if we had crossed over. When we had entered the project four years earlier, we had done so with the keen sense that God had placed us there. We were also fresh, energetic, and hungry for a challenge. Often in that final year we had to take our minds by the hand and walk them back to that instance when we detected that God was orchestrating that step of our lives. Only that vivid memory kept us going until the end.

The pressure became greater than any we'd known before. We survived finals! Finally the end of May arrived and we drove off to commencement with numb feelings and worn books, wearing well-pressed clothes and accompanied by well-pressed kids. Not until months later did we begin again to hear laughter in the home. It was such a relief to know that every day no longer had to be well-organized. That long, gnawing spell of our lives had passed, and we found our hearts still clutching each other . . . now with more tenacity than before. What was then bitter has again turned into a sweet and compelling memory.

How about you and your own past tough episodes? Have you taken time to go back and audit them to find the good that may have been brewing just below their turbulent, stormy surfaces? Have you been able to get beyond the mindset that hard times are tainted and useless, and that only good times have redeeming worth?

Candee and I have rummaged through so many of our tough memories just to find the merit they have had in cementing our soul-mated union. If you haven't thumbed back through your own, perhaps the time has come for you to do so. Who knows, you may unearth some treasures that will enhance the wealth of your own marriage and romance.

Sweet Experiences Made Sweeter

Not all memories spring from bitter experiences, thank the Lord! Many arise from occasions tagged with joy, pleasure, and good old fun. For Candee and me, simply hearing certain words or the mention of different names and places arrests our thoughts, calling them back to past moments when it was so good simply being together. The replaying of certain tapes or the hearing of certain musical scores can help to recall happenings where our souls were synchronized and our hearts were contented. You see, *yesterday's warmth is today's warmth relived and amplified without effort.* That is what happens with a sweet experience that slips gently into the future. It can and should be relived many times over—each time producing renewal and strength.

Weekend escapes, dinners by the bay, walks around the island or through the village, talks on the floor before a cozy fire, evenings with other coveted friends—these good experiences seem to keep on producing even warmer memories for us to relive in our own union. It's not so much the place or the activity that's important, but the discussions we have had while there, the comfort we have found at that moment by being in the other's presence, the dreams we have discovered in our minds that later took solid form. There are even roads we've driven and paths we have walked hundreds of times just because almost every time we have retraced them they've prompted something within us that doesn't transpire at home where our routines dominate.

Actually, both bitter and sweet experiences can have benefits for us, but usually the difference between the two is that the bitter ones happen apart from our control, the sweet ones develop because we are to a great extent in control—we've taken the time to think about them in advance so that we can avoid those words or deeds that may sour them.

Memory-Making Shoved Aside and Forgotten

I have found from counseling couples in crisis that they have ceased being together under those kinds of conditions and circumstances that tend to germinate positive memories . . . ones that can lighten the heavy atmosphere under which they are trying to live. Some of you have discovered that sometimes laughter is the best therapy for ill feelings. Others of you need to test that discovery for yourselves.

Sterility in a relationship may be fostered by an overly busy life. Times of sharing, playing, and dreaming have been replaced by a more frantic workload at home or at the office.

People who build their own homes often have found this to be true. Designing the layout, pouring the foundation, and framing the structure are all fun. The task is new. The early steps show nearly instant progress. But weeks become months; months become a year or two. Time passes and what happens? The charm is lost. One person ends up spending much more time than the other doing those things which are tedious and laborious but can't be set aside. Dreams become burdens and profits become barriers. What was intended to be fun and memorable actually has the reverse effect.

It takes time to make the fun kinds of memories, but too often one mate is anxiously waiting for the other to stop long enough to reorganize or recapture the friendship while the other is burning himself or herself out in adjunct and nonsharable activities. It's a sad scene when we share the same bed, pull mail from the same box, draw checks on the same account, bathe in the same tub, worship side by side . . . and all we know that's left in our lives is duty, boredom, and distance. A modern humorist, Sam Levenson, really understands the problem. Here is his observation:

> Love at first sight is easy to understand. It's when two people have been looking at each other for years it becomes a miracle.

Good, well-planned memories can help the miracle endure.

Dreams and Memories: Members of the Same Household

So many times dreams have been the forerunners of memories. Do you dream together? Or when one of you begins to dream, does the other shoot him down with criticism: "You never think realistically. You need to get more practical." Tragically, dreamers are discounted as if they possess some mild insanity. But dreaming is essential. It enlarges our vision; it can keep us from perishing, in fact.

When was the last time the two of you took time to dream,

to think through your own relationship and the future you'd like to carve out? Such mutual involvement is not a luxury. Neither is it a waste of time.

Floyd and Harriet Thatcher, in summarizing common reasons marriages deteriorate, refer to alternatives that can reverse the pattern. Within that context they talk about the excitement that comes to couples who regularly dream together:

> While it is true that almost all marriages begin with unrealistic expectations and dreams are dreamed that may be incapable of fulfillment in real-life marriage, we have come to feel . . . that this need not spell doom to a relationship. But a marriage is likely to recover from weak or unrealistic expectations only as a couple catches the excitement of dreaming together continually, year after year, year in and year out. For most of us this takes planned and calculated effort and constant practice. Possibly it may even be a bit mechanical at first, but in time it will become a way of life.[1]

Speaking of the miracle of a surviving relationship, they add:

> It's a miracle born out of dreams, hopes and expectations of two people who refuse to let their marriage become humdrum and dull, with no more resiliency than wet and soggy cardboard. Obviously, there are no pat answers, no heaven-sent formulas, that insure success. But for us, dreams and affirmations shared on a regular basis—talked out and written down—have brought excitement and freshness to our marriage, especially during the last fifteen years. We've done more new things and traveled to more new places than during all the earlier years. Not that it is easy. In fact, there are times when we're too angry and upset to dream, or to expect better things tomorrow. But then in time our better sides take over, and we feel reassured of its value once again.[2]

1. Floyd and Harriet Thatcher, *Long Term Marriage* (Waco, Tex.: Word Bocks, 1980), pp. 46-47.
2. Ibid., p. 47.

This has certainly been the case in our our own marital friendship. Once Candee and I began paying close attention to the relationship dreaming had to the quality of our home life, we realized a few things. When we dream, our home runs more smoothly, our relationship enjoys longer seasons of reduced tension, and our kids feel more comfortable in our presence. However, when we cease dreaming, we grow tired more easily, our endurance drops, our laughter turns to silence, and our delight fades into edginess.

We have dreamed more and more as the years have passed. Yet there came a time when we found ourselves highly frustrated because our dreaming outpaced our achievements. We were talking about the things we wished for vocationally, the places we wanted to live, the way we wanted each room to appear in its finished state, the directions we desired our children to take, the lives we wanted to make an impact on. Most every moment we were together, we were talking about the future. Why? In part, because we wanted our lives to have significance and our memories to count.

After a while our reaction was, "Let's get realistic and confine our discussions to the present." However, we finally understood that it makes little difference if many or most of our dreams don't materialize. The point is: If you do not dream a great deal, you are bound to achieve little; and if you don't dream some, then you will have nothing stimulating to pull your life along. You will lack both motivation and growth, inspiration and progress.

The pursuit of dreams results in the shaping of good memories, and our memories give glue to our relationships. What is their net effect on our marriage and home?

- They seem to hold our lives together.
- They encourage the weary to go a bit further.
- They help the tense to tolerate a tad more, to hang in there another hour, week, or year.
- They make bearable the times separations are unavoidable. And they enable us to feel inwardly warm when all of life outside our dwelling has grown cold and threatening.

If you're not a dreamer by nature, don't criticize those who are. Where would life and culture be apart from those rich in dreams and imaginations?

If you've got a mate who's challenged by looking at life's future possibilities, thank God! Don't fight them. Cultivate an appreciation for their qualities which you may not intrinsically understand. You see, apart from dreaming, we cannot generate the kinds of activities that produce enriched memories upon which our souls will feed in our old age.

The Ingredients of Well-Made Memories

Besides dreaming, there are several other components that help us make lasting and unerring remembrances. Too often they are overlooked.

Time. You can't hurry a memory that's hatching. Impatience will shatter a potentially intimate moment. You have to shove aside your deadlines and allow more of your times to remain open-ended. Hearts and affections don't like to be sandwiched between tightly scheduled activities. But in our crazy, fast-paced world, we seem to try to pack our days and weekends as full as possible, hurrying from this to that, quickly stopping here or there along the way. We tend to shortchange our contacts with each other. In particular, just about the time our souls are drawing alongside one another, off goes the wristwatch alarm, signaling us to get home, change clothes, and race off to the next event on the program.

In our own marriage, Candee and I have learned to keep the schedule simple and to give adequate time for the things we both need and want to do. We don't stack demands on top of each other the way we might have a few years ago. Why? Because doing so led to stress—and compelling memories aren't born under such strain.

Spontaneity. The longer we all live surrounded by traditions, structures, agendas, and schedules, the more comfortable we feel with them. At the same time we feel ill at ease with the instincts and impulses that periodically surge through us. Tragically, one of the characteristics of youthfulness we lose as we get older is our free-spiritedness—that inclination to do things and go places with little or no notice. We accept constraint in its place and gradually forget the fun of tossing our shoes aside and walking along the shoreline, or riding around on a balmy evening enjoying the wind on our faces. Remember those days? We quickly lose sight of the satisfaction of rowing across the lake at sunset or of enjoying a hastily prepared picnic in a quiet out-of-the-way spot.

What do you do with your spur-of-the-moment thoughts of doing something unique and unpredictable? How do you handle thoughts like, "Wouldn't it be fun to toss some clothes into a bag and escape for the weekend?" or "Why don't I surprise her with a sitter this evening so the two of us can slip away to be alone?" Problem is that too many of us hear those suggestions in our heads, but we subdue them and counsel ourselves, "You shouldn't be thinking that way at your age."

One of our friends, a father of three young adults, was picking up such signals and decided not to ignore them this time. From his office he called his daughter who was still living at home and said, "Pack Mom's clothes and have 'em ready by lunch. She thinks I'm taking her to a restaurant. However, I'm taking her to San Diego for the weekend as a surprise; I've just confirmed our reservations. By the way, sweetheart, keep it a secret. When I get home put our bags in the trunk of my car."

This gutsy guy decided to run the risk of being spontaneous. So what happened? His stunned lady found herself a part of what she later described as "the most pleasurable weekend" of their more than twenty-five years of marriage. Spontaneity paid off, resulting in a rediscovered sense of freedom and adventure. It punctured a heavy, negative tone which had come to characterize their relationship.

We can't always program memorable events weeks in advance. Sometimes we need to follow our instincts instead of sequestering them because "mature people don't do such flighty things." Admittedly there needs to be balance, for spontaneity doesn't fit with all occasions. There are times when structure is needed.

Planning. Few things are worse than heading off to a nice dinner or a favorite hotel, only to end up hopping from one establishment to another because the places you normally count on are all filled.

We learned the hard way. One night Candee and I decided to be spontaneous (but without covering all of our bases). Our hopes were so high . . . time away from it all was so direly needed. So we took a two-hour drive south to spend the night. We left town about eight P.M. and arrived at our favored destination only to find a glaring *no vacancy* sign greeting us. We tried a half-dozen other places before realizing the town was overrun by those playing in a weekend pro-golf tournament. Needless to say, the two-hour return trip was awkward. The anticipation which permeated our trip down quickly dried out during the disappointing drive home. We pulled into our driveway about two A.M.

Tough lesson! But the incident has not been repeated. The lesson: *When hungry hearts and high hopes are involved, don't subject them to an ill-planned time away.* Planning can save some memories from sudden death.

Courage. Another ingredient for building well-made memories is courage. This ingredient is particularly important when it comes to being creative, trying those things that are out of the ordinary. Many of us are truly afraid to step out of the ruts we've passively gotten ourselves into. We have become so familiar with the sterile walls of those ever-deepening grooves that the thought of something else actually scares us.

What is courage?

Ernest Hemingway called it "grace under pressure." In fact, both the planner of a special moment and the one who is being surprised each need to exercise courage of this sort to make the moment work right. That's just what we need ourselves at times when we are trying to split from the familiar and explore the new. We need to push ourselves, with God's help, beyond our safe borders of experience and expression. We need to gracefully explore places and activities which before have been unknown to us. We need to realize that life is more than vanilla-flavored traditions. You see, such attempts will give us new dimensions to our worlds and added refreshment to our marriages.

There is one more ingredient that serves the memory-making process.

Impracticality. If we all waited to have children until we could afford them, perhaps the world would be a sparsely populated globe. Many things are like that, memory-building included. Always putting things into strict dollars-and-cents terms makes life dull . . . though most of the time it's wise for us to do so.

Budgets are lifesaving structures that keep us from sure financial disaster. However, there are times when making adjustments to the operating plan—moving dollars around—is preferable, especially if one or both of us needs to get away or if a special time alone with the children would make a gigantic difference in the mood within the homestead.

Look back through your heart-warming moments. Weren't many, if not the majority of them sponsored by bucks once designated for more serious, "responsible" things like soaps and cleansers, tires and brakes, lawn fertilizers and exterior paints? Those things can usually wait another month or three. (Some of you are saying, "That's already what's happening and we are still coming up short!") Our relationships can't wait. In fact, the relationship usually gets the leftover portions of both our time and money. Isn't that sad? They usually defer to everything else. No wonder they become boring and lifeless with time.

Please, keep your memory-making efforts alive. One day you won't remember all the stuff you went without, but you will remember the good times you had together.

Being impractical can reach into other realms also. For example, there are times it might be okay to leave mildly sick children home with a sitter, or to have someone come in a few hours to watch the elderly parent you are nursing in your own home. These kinds of situations can last for months, and at the same time a marital relationship can be severely neglected. Even in times like these, you need brief breaks to maintain the spark of a relationship.

I mention this to you, having a particular situation in mind. One couple I have watched over the years became so buried by the problems and pressures of raising multiple young children that their relationship with each other subtly wasted away in the process. From one November through the following February it seemed that the children were continuously ill, trading and repeating viral infections and colds as if they had conspired against their mom and dad's marriage. The fledgling mother felt she could never leave sick children with someone else, because to do so was to be irresponsible. She was so conscientious that even the thought of breaking away caused her to feel guilty.

So for months, every date her husband had planned with her was canceled mere hours before they were to leave. She wanted to go, yet always thought she must stay home under the circumstances. Actually, she wasn't sure what was the right thing to do, and she worried how others, including her parents, would interpret her leaving.

It wasn't until the union became horribly distressed that the wife realized both she and her husband needed some play time together. She found that several hour breaks, scattered throughout the siege, would have in fact made her hospital an easier one to attend. She had to decide to be a little "impractical" here and there so that they could bridge their hearts on the other side of town, away from their sick darlings.

It wasn't until her husband threatened to leave their lifeless and boring marriage that she came to terms with the necessity of getting away from the relentless demands of the family. She not only needed to nurse the little ones she loved, but also her relationship with her husband.

Such timely breaks can invigorate us. We need them frequently. And if it means struggling to get them, then we must do that. We cannot grow together if we do not spend time together.

The Effects of Well-Made Memories on Our Lives

For those who are young, shared memories help fortify the motivation to keep on going, even when hardship mounts.

Shared memories cause young folk to work harder, to love more diligently, and to play more often. However, there's an incomparable effect they can have upon those who are older. Solomon addresses the matter in these words:

> Here is what I have seen to be good and fitting: to eat, to drink and enjoy oneself [literally, "see good"] in all one's labor in which he toils under the sun during the few years of his life which God has given him; for this is his reward. Furthermore, as for every man to whom God has given riches and wealth, He has also empowered him to eat from them and to receive his reward and rejoice in his labor; this is the gift of God. For he will not often consider the years of his life [literally, "his age"], because God keeps him occupied with the gladness of his heart [or "past memories"] (Ecclesiastes 5:18-20).

The point Solomon made is that when one is elderly, he or she will not be preoccupied with his age because God will keep him focused on the warm memories of his past. Of course, this presupposes that good memories were nurtured and cultivated along the way.

I wish I could convey to every couple the necessity of building solid, compelling, positive, and warm memories in their early years together. Life goes by so rapidly. Really we have no time to waste allowing poor ones to germinate. And doing this is a shared responsibility.

We tend to be more concerned about saving money for those retirement years than we are with saving memories. However, we must come to grips with the fact that it's not our bucks that will keep us cushioned and comfortable in our older years, but those treasured memories we took the time to establish.

I'd like to ask you to guard your memories carefully. If you haven't been doing that, begin taking charge of those patterns and activities now. Own the responsibility in joint tenancy. Keep on asking yourselves, How do we want this one to turn out? Can we avoid disappointment and preserve our delight? Are we taking the time to put together remembrances that will not only be ours in the future, but which we can also give away to our offspring as part of the heritage we intend to give them and their children?

There is no better time for you to turn this matter of your lives over to God than right now. He's anxious to help you repair your painful memories and to sustain this valuable dimension of your homelife.

Reflection

The priority of building and reliving memories can be traced all the way back to the heart of God.

Often it's the bitter experiences turned sweet that have the greatest impact on our relationships.

Sharing positive memories helps motivate us to keep on going, to work harder at our unions, to love more diligently, and to play more often.

Steps for Marital Growth

- As Thomas Fuller said, "That which is bitter to endure may be sweet to remember." Identify the turning point in your mind that allowed a bitter memory to become sweet.
- List shared activities . . . good memories . . . things that somehow have fallen to the side. How can you renew some of those activities?
- Sometimes laughter is the best therapy for pain—physical or emotional. Think about the last time you allowed yourself to laugh with your mate, forgetting the pressures hanging over your heads. Do you laugh less these days or more? If less, why? What is it you are afraid letting go will do to you?
- As you review the ingredients of well-made memories: time, spontaneity, planning, courage, and impracticality, ask yourself the following questions: With which do you have the greatest difficulty? Which one does your mate find most troublesome? What can you do to work on it?

Pleasant memories take time to cultivate and good marriages are crafted by today's choices. Are you making choices *today* that will encourage you and your mate to grow apart, or are you making choices today to grow together as two friends in love?